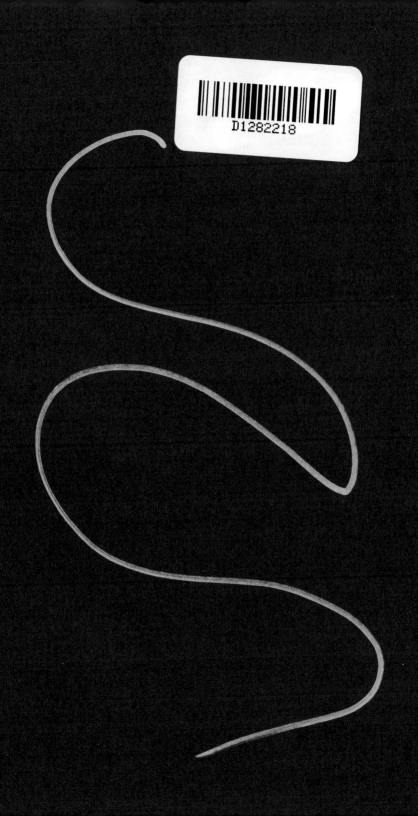

D1282218

Igor Fedorovitch Stravinsky, 1882-1971;
A Practical Guide to Publications of His Music

Tom Ahrens

Igor Fedorovitch Stravinsky, 1882-1971;
A Practical Guide to Publications of His Music
by Dominique-Rene de Lerma
assisted by Thomas J. Ahrens

The Kent State University Press

Library of Congress Cataloging in Publication Data

De Lerma, Dominique-René.
 Igor Fedorovitch Stravinsky, 1882-1971.

  1. Stravinskiĭ, Igor' Fedorovich, 1882-1971—
Bibliography.   I. Ahrens, Thomas J.   joint author.
ML134.S96D44   016.78'092'4   74-79152
ISBN 0-87338-158-0

Copyright 1974 by Dominique-Rene de Lerma.
All rights reserved.
Library of Congress Catalog Card Number 74-79152.
ISBN 0-87338-158-0.
Printed in the United States of America.
First edition.

In honor of Leopold Stokowski
with his gracious permission

Contents

Preface

The purpose of this bibliography is to list the publications
of music by Igor Stravinsky, including within each entry that
information beneficial to librarians and students for the
identification of the composer's complete works and their
publication sources. It is primarily a register of the publications,
to which is added supplemental data that may serve auxiliary
functions. This is then a counterpart to my study on the music
of Ives,[1] with modifications within the entries and indexes
which were thought appropriate.

   The information presented here was gathered from a variety
of sources. As would be essential with any bibliographic
survey, the holdings of the Library of Congress and of the
New York Public Library were examined. The acquisitional
projects I initiated in 1963, when I became music librarian at
Indiana University, included from the start the development

---

[1] *Charles Edward Ives, 1874-1954; a bibliography of his music.* Kent: Kent
State University Press, 1970. xi + 212pp.

of as complete a collection of all editions of Stravinsky's music
as was possible. The fact that these libraries, among the five
largest music collections in the United States, did not have all
of the publications provided evidence of the need for the
present summary.

The catalogs of Stravinsky's publishers were consulted,
as were references to his *oeuvre* in major biographical studies
and critiques. Of primary importance among these is Eric
Walter White's *Stravinsky; the composer and his works*
(Berkeley & Los Angeles: University of California Press, 1966).

This listing bears evidence of advice and assistance from
James Elrod, former associate music librarian at Indiana
University, and from David E. Fenske, who now holds that
position. My former secretary, Mrs. Sharon B. Thompson,
provided extensive direct and auxiliary assistance. Plate numbers
and publication dates were rechecked by José Piedra, and the
entire manuscript in its last draft was reviewed by Roy Whelden.
My sincere appreciation is also offered representatives of
those publishing firms who verified the data and provided
information on those publications which were not within the
holdings of the three major libraries consulted. Additional
gratitude is due the administrative personnel of the Kent State
University Press (Paul Rohmann, director; Howard Allen,
former director; Mrs. Jo Zuppan, former editor, and
Michael Di Battista, editor) for the support, guidance and
encouragement they have given me in this project, as well as
others.

Finally, I wish to express my appreciation to radio station
WTTS in Bloomington (for reasons it never anticipated),
and to my faithful colleague, whose interest and friendship
began with this project: Thomas J. Ahrens.

D.S.L.
Naples, Florida
31 December 1972

Introduction

The worksheet format employed in this project was originally designed for application in similar research on the works of Béla Bartók, which project has been indefinitely suspended. It subsequently was employed on my extensive bio-bibliographical research on *Black music; a preliminary register of the composers and their works,* yet in progress. The worksheet provides space for registration of the following elements:

1. *Uniform title.* Titles of compositions are entered by this form, no doubt familiar to patrons of most American music libraries.[2] This has been amplified as needed to specify the particular version involved in a manner akin to the practice of the New York Public Library and that of Indiana University. In this manner one may readily determine that *Le chant du*

---

[2] *Anglo-American cataloging rules; North-American text.* Chicago: American Library Association, 1967.

rossignol; piano is a version of that work prepared for piano by the composer himself, whereas *Octet, winds; arr., piano* indicates the piano reduction is by a second individual. Cross-references are made from variant titles (based on publications) to the main entry when such a process is thought to be of functional value to librarians.

2. *Index number.* Each main entry is assigned an index number consisting of the alphabetic incipit and an Arabic numeral designation which places like entries alphabetically within an arbitrarily established hierarchical order. In order to include *Canon, orchestra* within the alphabetical listing, it becomes necessary to regard the index number as a decimal. That work, which has not been examined, thus becomes C0.5 and appears before C1.

3. *Medium.* This indication is based essentially on that terminology provided in *Music subject headings used on printed catalog cards of the Library of Congress*,[3] which accounts for the use of plurals within the main entry as reference to a single title.

4. *Poet.* The name forms of those individuals responsible for a text, indicated here, have not been verified for library use.

5. *Year.* The date cited is that in which the work was completed.

6. *Alternate title.* Variant titles, including translations, are noted here.

7. *Duration.* The performance time of the work is registered when indicated by the composer or his publisher. When different timings have been given by the publishers, only one has been cited, arbitrarily selected. The duration will naturally be subject to variation in actual performance.

---

[3] *Music subject headings used on printed catalog cards of the Library of Congress.* Washington: Library of Congress, Subject Cataloging Division, 1952.

8. *Notes.* Any pertinent bibliographic factor not suitable for inclusion elsewhere is mentioned here.

9. *Commission.* Here is cited those individuals or groups responsible for *scritture* when these have been ascertained.

10. *Dedication.*

11. *First performance.* City, hall, performers and date are cited as this information has been readily available.

12. *Contents.* Titles of items within composite works are registered when this may be of identification assistance.

13. *Published.* The register of imprints includes the publisher, year of issue, series, plate number, notes relative to the specific publication, and the number applicable to Library of Congress catalog cards, as determined. Any element within this group not provided was unavailable from the three major libraries whose holdings were checked, from the publisher in question, and from other references examined during ten years of research.

Supplementary points of entry are provided by the publisher, medium, proper name and chronological indexes.

The only titles intentionally eliminated from this register are those works arranged for player piano for which no printed version appears to have been published.

To facilitate typesetting, the ligatures of transliterated Cyrillic have not been included.

Research on this bibliography was terminated on May 14, 1974.

Bibliography

Works by Stravinsky

A1 *Abraham and Isaac*
   Medium: Cantatas; Songs (Medium voice) with
      chamber orchestra
   Poet: Biblical text
   Year: 1963
   Duration: 12'
   Dedication: "To the people of the state of Israel"
   First performance: Jerusalem; Ephraim Biran, baritone;
      Robert Craft, conductor; 23 August 1964
   Published: (1) Boosey & Hawkes, 1965, plate no. B&H
      19197, full score, LC 65-54350/M; (2) Boosey &
      Hawkes, 1965 (Hawkes pocket scores, 762)

A2 *Abraham and Isaac. Piano-vocal score*
   Medium: Piano-vocal scores; Songs (Medium voice)
      with piano

Published: (1) Boosey & Hawkes, 1965, plate no. B&H
19162, LC 65-54349/M

A3 *Agon*
Medium: Ballets; Orchestral music
Year: 1957
Duration: 20'
Dedication: Lincoln Kirstein and George Balanchine
First performance: Los Angeles; Robert Craft, conductor;
17 June 1957
Published: (1) Boosey & Hawkes, 1957, full score,
LC M57-2110; (2) Boosey & Hawkes, 1957 (Hawkes
pocket scores, 701) plate no. B&H 18336, LC M57-2110;
(3) Muzyka, 1972, published with *Orpheus*

A4 *Agon; 2 pianos*
Medium: Piano music (2 pianos)
Published: (1) Boosey & Hawkes, 1957, plate no. B&H
18337, LC M58-121

Aldous Huxley in memoriam
see *Variations, orchestra* (V3)

Anthem
see *The dove descending breaks the air* (D5)

A5 *Apollon musagète*
Medium: Ballets; String-orchestra music
Year: 1928
First performance: Washington, D. C.; 27 April 1928
Published: (1) Edition Russe de Musique, 1928, plate no.
RMV 441, LC 41-M6812

A6 *Apollon musagète; piano*
Medium: Piano music
Year: 1928

Published: (1) Edition Russe de Musique, 1928, plate no.
RMV 441, LC M56-216

A7 *Apollon musagète (1947)*
Medium: Ballets; String-orchestra music
Year: 1947
Published: (1) Boosey & Hawkes, Edition Russe de Musique,
1949, plate no. B&H 16213, full score, LC 49-28998;
(2) Boosey & Hawkes, 1949 (Hawkes pocket scores,
611) plate no. B&H 16213

Les augures printaniers
see *Le sacre du printemps. Les augures printaniers;
arr., piano* (S4)

A8 *Ave Maria*
Medium: Choruses (Mixed voices), Unaccompanied
Year: 1934
Alternate title: *Bogoroditse Dievo*
Duration: 1'
Notes: Text in Slavonic
Published: (1) Edition Russe de Musique, 1934, plate no.
RMV 582; (2) Boosey & Hawkes, 1969

A9 *Ave Maria (1949)*
Medium: Choruses (Mixed voices), Unaccompanied
Year: 1949
Notes: Text in Latin
Published: (1) Boosey & Hawkes, 1949 (Winthrop Rogers
church choral series, 28) plate no. 1832

B1 *Babel*
Medium: Cantatas; Choruses (Men's voices) with orchestra
Poet: Biblical text
Year: 1944

Duration: 7'

Notes: Designed as the seventh item within a composite
work to be known as *Genesis*, consisting of (1) *Prelude*,
by Arnold Schönberg; (2) *Creation*, by Nathaniel
Schilkret; (3) *Fall of man*, by Alexandre Tansman;
(4) *Cain and Abel*, by Darius Milhaud; (5) *Flood*,
by Mario Castelnuovo-Tedesco; (6) *Covenant*, by Ernst
Toch, (7) *Babel*, by Igor Stravinsky; other contributions
were to have been composed by Béla Bartók, Paul
Hindemith, and Serge Prokofiev; English text by
Ludwig Anders

Commission: Nathaniel Schilkret

First performance: Los Angeles; Ebell Theater; Werner
Janssen, conductor; 18 November 1945

Published: (1) B. Schott's Söhne, Associated Music
Publishers, 1953 (Edition Schott, 4412) plate no. BSS
37844a, in English; (2) B. Schott's Söhne, 1953, plate no.
BSS 37844, in English with German translation by
Ludwig Anders

B2 *Babel. Piano-vocal score*

Medium: Piano-vocal scores; Choruses (Men's voices)
with piano; Cantatas

Published: (1) B. Schott's Söhne, Associated Music
Publishers, 1952 (Edition Schott, 4342) plate no.
BSS 37846, LC M54-2099rev

Baïka

see *Renard* (R7)

B3 *Le baiser de la fée*

Medium: Ballets; Orchestral music

Year: 1928

Alternate title: *The fairy's kiss*

Duration: 45'

Notes: Based on music by Peter Tschaikowsky
Dedication: In memoriam Peter Tschaikowsky
First performance: Paris; Opéra; Ballet Ida Rubenstein;
   Igor Stravinsky, conductor; 27 November 1928
Contents: Four scenes
Published: (1) Edition Russe de Musique, 1928,
   plate no. RMV 455

B4 *Le baiser de la fée; piano*
   Medium: Piano music
   Published: (1) Edition Russe de Musique, 1928,
      plate no. RMV 455

B5 *Le baiser de la fée (1950)*
   Medium: Ballets; Orchestral music
   Year: 1950
   Published: (1) Boosey & Hawkes, Edition Russe de Musique,
      1952, full score; (2) Boosey & Hawkes, 1952 (Hawkes
      pocket scores, 679) plate no. B&H 16669

B6 *Le baiser de la fée (1950); piano*
   Medium: Piano music
   Contents: (1) The lullaby in the storm (Berceuse de la
      tempête); (2) A village fête (Une fête au village);
      (3) At the mill (Au moulin); (4) Scene (Scène);
      (5) The lullaby of the land beyond time and place
      (Berceuse des demeures éternelles)
   Published: (1) Boosey & Hawkes, 1954, plate no. B&H
      17561, LC M54-2556

   Le baiser de la fée (Divertimento)
   see *Le baiser de la fée (Suite)* (B7)

B7 *Le baiser de la fée (Suite)*
Medium: Orchestral music
Year: 1934
Alternate title: (1) *Divertimento*; (2) *Le baiser de la fée (Divertimento)*
Duration: 20'
Contents: (1) Sinfonia; (2) Danses suisses; (3) Scherzo; (4) Pas de deux: adagio, variations, coda
Published: (1) Edition Russe de Musique, 1938, plate no. RMV 642; (2) Boosey & Hawkes, full score; (3) Boosey & Hawkes (Hawkes pocket scores, 665)

B8 *Le baiser de la fée (Suite); violin & piano*
Medium: Violin and piano music
Year: 1932
Notes: Arranged by the composer and Samuel Dushkin
Contents: (1) Sinfonia; (2) Danses suisses; (3) Scherzo; (4) Pas de deux
Published: (1) Edition Russe de Musique, 1934, plate no. RMV 592-593, 595-596; (2) Boosey & Hawkes, 1934, plate no. B&H 17269; (3) Gosudarstvennyi Muzykal'noe izd-vo, 1963

B9 *Le baiser de la fée (Suite, 1949)*
Medium: Orchestral music
Year: 1949
Alternate title: (1) *Divertimento*; (2) *Le baiser de la fée (Divertimento)*
Contents: (1) Sinfonia; (2) Danses suisses; (3) Scherzo; (4) Pas de deux
Published: (1) Boosey & Hawkes, 1950 (Hawkes pocket scores, 665) plate no. B&H 16669

B10 *Le baiser de la fée. Deuxième tableau. Selection;*
violin & piano (1934)
   Medium: Violin and piano music
   Year: 1934
   Alternate title: (1) *Ballad*
   Notes: Arranged by the composer and Samuel Dushkin
   Published: (1) Edition Russe de Musique, 1934,
      plate no. B&H 17269

B11 *Le baiser de la fée. Deuxième tableau. Selection;*
violin & piano (1951)
   Medium: Violin and piano music
   Year: 1951
   Notes: Arranged by the composer and Jeanne Gautier
   Published: (1) Boosey & Hawkes, 1951, plate no. B&H
      17816, LC M54-2107; (2) Muzyka, 1971

Ballad
   see *Le baiser de la fée. Deuxième tableau. Selection;*
      violin & piano (1934) (B10)

Basle concerto
   see *Concerto, string orchestra, D* (C39)

Berceuse
   see also entries for *L'oiseau de feu* (O13-O22)

B12 *Berceuse*
   Medium: Songs with piano
   Poet: Igor Stravinsky
   Year: 1917
   Duration: 45''
   Notes: French text by C. F. Ramuz
   Dedication: Ludmilla Stravinsky

B13 *Berceuses du chat*
    Medium: Songs (Low voice) with 3 clarinets
    Poet: After popular Russian texts
    Year: 1916
    Alternate titles: (1) *Cat's cradle song*; (2) *Katzenlieder*
    Duration: 5'
    Notes: French text by C. F. Ramuz, German text by
      R. St. Hoffmann
    Dedication: Natalie Gontcharova and Michel Larionov
    Contents: (1) Sur le poêle (Hinterm Herd; Spi koty);
      (2) Interieur (Katzenidylle; Kogy ma pechi); (3) Dodo
      (Wiegenlied; Baĭ-baĭ); (4) Ce qu'il a le chat (Was
      gehört der Katz; U kota kota)
    Published: (1) Ad. Henn, 1917, LC M53-313; (2) J. & W.
      Chester, 1917 (Chester library) plate no. W.Ph.V.
      292/J.W.C. 14a; (3) B. Schott's Söhne
      (Edition Schott, 3466)

B14 *Berceuses du chat; voice & piano*
    Medium: Songs with piano
    Published: (1) Ad. Henn, 1923, plate no. A.68H.;
      (2) B. Schott's Söhne (Edition Schott, 2054)

Bogoroditse Dievo
    see *Ave Maria* (A8)

La bonne chanson
    see *Poèmes de Verlaine, op. 9* (P45)

Boris Godunov
    see Z11

C0.5 *Canon, orchestra*
    Medium: Orchestral music
    Published: (1) Boosey & Hawkes, 1973.

Canon, 2 tenors
    see *Little canon* (L1)

C1 *Canon on a Russian popular theme*
    Medium: Orchestral music
    Year: 1965
    Duration: 30″
    Notes: Based on finale of *L'oiseau de feu* (O8)
    First performance: Toronto; CBC Symphony Orchestra;
      Robert Craft, conductor
    Published: (1) Boosey & Hawkes, 1965

C2 *Canons, 2 horns*
    Medium: Horn music (2 horns)
    Year: 1917
    Dedication: Dr. Roux, of Genève

C3 *Cantata*
    Medium: Cantatas
    Year: 1952
    Duration: 30′
    Dedication: Los Angeles Chamber Symphony Society
    First performance: Los Angeles Chamber Symphony
      Society; 11 November 1952
    Contents: (1) A lyke-wake dirge I; (2) Ricercar I; (3) A
      lyke-wake dirge II; (4) Ricercar II; (5) A lyke-wake
      dirge III; (6) Westron wind; (7) A lyke-wake dirge IV
    Published: (1) Boosey & Hawkes, 1952 (Hawkes pocket
      scores, 666) plate no. B&H 17245, LC M54-1785

C4 *Cantata. Piano-vocal score*
    Medium: Cantatas; Piano-vocal scores
    Published: (1) B. Schott's Söhne, Associated Music
      Publishers, 1937, plate no. BSS 34890; (2) Boosey &
      Hawkes, 1952, plate no. B&H 17247, LC M54-1767

14

C5 *Canticum sacrum*
Medium: Cantatas
Year: 1955
Alternate title: *Canticum sacrum ad honorem
Sancti Marci nominis*
First performance: Venice; San Marco; Igor Stravinsky,
conductor; 13 September 1956
Contents: (1) Dedicato; Euntes in mundum; (2) Surge,
aquilo; (3) Ad Ares virtutes horationes; (4) Brevis motus
cantilenae; (5) Illi autem profecti
Published: (1) Boosey & Hawkes, 1956 (Hawkes pocket
scores, 691) plate no. B&H 18168, LC M57-439;
(2) Boosey & Hawkes, 1956, full score, LC M57-667

C6 *Canticum sacrum. Piano-vocal score*
Medium: Cantatas; Piano-vocal scores
Published: (1) Boosey & Hawkes, 1956, plate no.
B&H 18169

Canticum sacrum ad honorem Sancti Marci nominis
see *Canticum sacrum* (C5)

Cantique
see *Etudes, orchestra. No. 3: Cantique; arr., organ* (E10)

Canzonetta
see Z14

C7 *Capriccio, piano & orchestra*
Medium: Piano with orchestra
Year: 1929
Duration: 20′
Notes: Also published in *Sochineniia dlia fortepiano* (W2)
First performance: Paris; Salle Pleyel; Paris Symphony
Orchestra; Ernest Ansermet, conductor; Igor Stravinsky,
piano; 6 December 1929
Published: (1) Edition Russe de Musique, 1930

C8 *Capriccio, piano & orchestra; 2 pianos*
  Medium: Piano music (2 pianos)
  Published: (1) Edition Russe de Musique, 1930, plate no.
    R.M.V. 470, LC 61-2188

C9 *Capriccio, piano & orchestra (1949)*
  Medium: Piano with orchestra
  Year: 1949
  Published: (1) Boosey & Hawkes, 1952 (Hawkes pocket
    scores, 610) LC M54-1919

C10 *Capriccio, piano & orchestra (1949); 2 pianos*
  Medium: Piano music (2 pianos)
  Year: 1949
  Published: (1) Boosey & Hawkes, 1952, plate no. B&H
    16990, LC 52-65740

  A card game
  see *The card party* (C11)

C11 *The card party*
  Medium: Ballets
  Year: 1936
  Alternate title: (1) *A card game*; (2) *Jeu de cartes*; (3) *Das
    Kartenspiel*
  Duration: 23'
  First performance: New York; Metropolitan Opera House;
    American Ballet; Igor Stravinsky, conductor;
    27 April 1937
  Contents: 3 deals
  Published: (1) B. Schott's Söhne, Associated Music
    Publishers, 1937 (Edition Schott, 3511) plate no. BSS
    35036; (2) B. Schott's Söhne, 1937 (Edition Schott 56)
    plate no. BSS 34888, full score

C12 *The card party; piano*
   Medium: Piano music
   Published: (1) B. Schott's Söhne, Associated Music
      Publishers, 1937 (Edition Schott, 3296) plate no. BSS
      34890

La carriera d'un libertino
   see *The rake's progress* (R3)

Cat's cradle song
   see *Berceuses du chat* (B13)

Chanson de la mère
   see *Mavra. Net' ne zabyt'; voice & piano* (M8)

Chanson de Parasha
   see entries for *Mavra. Drug moĭ milyĭ* (M5-M7)

Chanson russe
   see entries for *Mavra. Drug moĭ milyĭ* (M5-M7)

Chant des bateliers du Volga
   see Z5

C13 *Le chant du rossignol*
   Medium: Orchestral music
   Year: 1917
   Alternate title: (1) *The song of the nightingale;* (2) *Piesnia
      solovyia*
   Duration: 20'
   Notes: Based on music earlier used in *Le rossignol* (R13)
   First performance: Genève; Orchestra de la Suisse
      Romande; Ernest Ansermet, conductor; 1 December 1919
   Published: (1) Edition Russe de Musique, 1921, 22 cm.,
      LC 61-2089; (2) Edition Russe de Musique, 1921,
      21 cm., LC M61-2077; (3) Boosey & Hawkes, 1921
      (Hawkes pocket scores, 633) plate no. B&H 16312

C14 *Le chant du rossignol; piano*
    Medium: Piano music
    Published: (1) Edition Russe de Musique, 1927, plate no.
       R.M.V. 422; (2) Boosey & Hawkes

C15 *Le chant du rossignol. Marche chinoise; arr., piano*
    Medium: Piano music
    Notes: Arranged by Frederick Block
    Published: (1) Marks Music Corporation, 1941
       (Kaleidoscope edition, 11502) LC 70-231251; (2) Marks
       Music Corporation, 1936 (Album of Stravinsky
       masterpieces; contemporary masterpieces, v. 9)

C16 *Le chant du rossignol. Selections; violin & piano*
    Medium: Violin and piano music
    Year: 1932
    Notes: Arranged by the composer and Samuel Dushkin
    Contents: (1) Air du rossignol; (2) Marche chinoise
    Published: (1) Edition Russe de Musique, 1934, plate no.
       R.M.V. 583; (2) Boosey & Hawkes

C17 *Chant funèbre sur la morte de Rimsky-Korsakov, op. 5*
    Medium: Band music
    Year: 1908
    Alternate title: *Funeral dirge*
    Notes: Lost
    Dedication: In memoriam Rimsky-Korsakov
    First performance: St. Petersburg; Felix Blumenfeld,
      conductor; 1908

C18 *Chants russes*
    Medium: Songs with piano
    Poet: After popular Russian texts
    Year: 1919
    Alternate title: *Russian songs*

Duration: 5'45"

Notes: Nos. 1 and 2 also appear in his *Songs* (S25) as nos. 1
and 2; French translation by C. F. Ramuz

Dedication: Béla and Maja de Strozzi-Pečić

Contents: (1) Canard; ronde (Sekezeny; khorovodnaia);
(2) Chanson pour compter (Zapievnaia); (3) Le moineau
est assis (Podliudnaia); (4) Chant dissident (Septantskaia)

Published: (1) J. & W. Chester, 1923, 1920, plate no.
JWC 3831

C19 *Church prayer*
Year: 1930 ca.
Notes: Unfinished

C20 *Les cinq doigts*
Medium: Piano music
Year: 1921
Duration: 8'
Notes: Subsequently arr. for winds and strings with changed
order of movements as *Instrumental miniatures* (*see* I3)
Contents: (1) Andantino; (2) Allegro; (3) Allegretto; (4)
Larghetto; (5) Moderato; (6) Lento; (7) Vivo; (8) Pesante
Published: (1) J. & W. Chester, 1922 (Chester series, 100)
plate no. J&WC 2090, LC 68-42501/M

C21 *Les cinq doigts; arr., 2 guitars*
Medium: Guitar music (2 guitars)
Notes: Arranged by Theodore Norman
Published: (1) J. & W. Chester, 1969, LC 71-212524

C21.5 *Les cinq doigts. No. 2: Allegro; arr., guitar*
Medium: Guitar music
Notes: Arranged by Theodore Norman
Published: (1) J. & W. Chester

C22 *Les cinq doigts. No. 8: Pesante, instrumental ensemble*
  Medium: Instrumental ensembles
  Year: 1961
  Notes: Withdrawn, replaced by *Instrumental miniatures*
    (*see* I3)
  First performance: Mexico City; Robert Craft, conductor;
    December 1961

C23 *Circus polka, piano*
  Medium: Piano music
  Year: 1942
  Duration: 4'
  Published: (1) Associated Music Publishers, 1942, plate no.
    AS 194219, LC 79-229083; (2) B. Schott's Söhne, 1951
    (Edition Schott, 4282) plate no. BSS 37841

C24 *Circus polka, piano; orchestra*
  Medium: Orchestral music
  Year: 1942
  Duration: 4'
  Commission: Ringling Brothers, Barnum and Baily Circus
  First performance: Boston; Sanders Theatre; Boston
    Symphony Orchestra; Igor Stravinsky, conductor;
    13 January 1944
  Published: (1) B. Schott's Söhne, 1952, 1944 (Edition Schott,
    4274) plate no. BSS 38096, LC 44-49228; (2) Associated
    Music Publishers, 1944 (Edition Schott, 4274)
    plate no. AS 194343

C25 *Circus polka, piano; arr., band*
  Medium: Band music
  Year: 1942
  Duration: 4'
  Notes: Arranged by David Reskin

First performance: New York; Madison Square Garden;
Ringling Brothers, Barnum and Baily Circus Band;
Merle Evans, conductor; 1942
Published: (1) Associated Music Publishers, 1948,
LC 48-21061

C26 *Circus polka, piano; arr., 2 pianos*
Medium: Piano music (2 pianos)
Notes: Arranged by Victor Babin
Published: (1) Associated Music Publishers, 1943, plate
no. AS 194225-12; (2) Schott (London) (Edition
Schott, 4283) plate no. BSS 10155

C27 *Circus polka, piano; arr., violin & piano*
Medium: Violin and piano music
Year: 1942
Notes: Arranged by Sol Babitz
Published: (1) Associated Music Publishers, 1943, plate
no. AS 194226; (2) B. Schott's Söhne, 1943, LC
45-17690

Con queste paroline
see *Pulcinella. Con queste paroline; voice & piano* (P63.5)

C28 *Concerto, string quartet*
Medium: String quartets
Year: 1920
Duration: 6'

Dedication: Flonzaley Quartet
Published: (1) Wilhelm Hansen, 1923, plate no. 18294;
(2) Wilhelm Hansen, 1951 (Wilhelm Hansen edition,
2359) revised and ed. Julia A. Burt, score plate no. 18294,
parts plate no. 18295; (3) Muzyka, 1968, includes his
Pièces for string quartet LC 68-130660/M

C29 *Concertino, string quartet; piano, 4 hands*
  Medium: Piano music (4 hands)
  Year: 1920
  Notes: Reduction by the composer, revised and edited by
    Julia A. Burt
  Published: (1) Wilhelm Hansen, 1925 (Wilhelm Hansen
    edition, 2490) plate no. 18844

C30 *Concertino, string quartet; winds & strings*
  Medium: Instrumental ensembles
  Year: 1952
  Duration: 6'
  First performance: Los Angeles; Los Angeles Chamber
    Symphony Orchestra; 11 November 1952
  Published: (1) Wilhelm Hansen, 1953 (Wilhelm Hansen
    edition, 3962b) plate no. 27104b, score, LC M54-2161;
    (2) Wilhelm Hansen, 1953 (Wilhelm Hansen edition,
    3962a) plate no. 27104a, parts

C31 *Concertino, string quartet; arr., piano*
  Medium: Piano music
  Notes: Arranged by Arthur Lourié
  Published: (1) Wilhelm Hansen, 1925 (Wilhelm Hansen
    edition, 2397) plate no. 18575

C32 *Concerto, chamber orchestra, E flat*
  Medium: Chamber-orchestra music
  Year: 1938
  Alternate title: *Dumbarton Oaks*
  Duration: 12'
  Commission: Mr. & Mrs. Robert Woods Bliss
  First performance: Washington; Nadia Boulanger,
    conductor; 8 May 1938
  Contents: (1) Tempo giusto; (2) Allegretto; (3) Con moto

St. Peter's College Library
St. Peter's College, Jersey City, N. J. 07306

Published: (1) B. Schott's Söhne, 1938 (Edition Schott,
2851) full score, LC 65-41856/M; (2) B. Schott's Söhne,
1938 (Edition Schott, 3527) plate no. 35383a,
miniature score, LC 44-49155rev2/M; (3) Associated
Music Publishers, 1938 (Edition Schott, 3527) miniature
score; (4) Muzyka, 1971, in *Kamernye ansambli* (W1)

C33 *Concerto, Chamber orchestra, E flat; 2 pianos*
Medium: Piano music (2 pianos)
Published: (1) B. Schott's Söhne, 1938 (Edition Schott,
2791) plate no. BSS 35561, LC 47-39604rev/M;
(2) Associated Music Publishers, 1938
(Edition Schott, 2791)

C34 *Concerto, piano & band*
Medium: Piano with band
Year: 1924
Duration: 20'
Notes: Ed. Albert Spaulding; also published in
Sochineniia dlia fortepiano
Dedication: Natalie Koussevitsky
First performance: Paris; Concerts Koussevitsky; Serge
Koussevitsky, conductor; Igor Stravinsky, piano;
22 May 1924
Contents: (1) Largo; allegro; (2) Larghissimo; (3) Allegro
Published: (1) Edition Russe de Musique, 1936,
LC 68-42500/M; (2) Edition Russe de Musique, 1924,
plate no. RMV 414

C35 *Concerto, piano & band (1950)*
Medium: Piano with band
Year: 1950
Duration: 20'
Published: (1) Boosey & Hawkes, 1960 (Hawkes pocket
scores, 724) plate no. B&H 18766, LC M60-2872

C36 *Concerto, piano & band; 2 pianos*
  Medium: Piano music (2 pianos)
  Year: 1924
  Published: (1) Edition Russe de Musique, 1924,
    plate no. RMV 1; (2) Boosey & Hawkes, 1947, plate no.
    B&H 16329, ed. Albert Spaulding

C37 *Concerto, piano & band. Largo; piano*
  Medium: Piano music

C38 *Concerto, 2 pianos, unaccompanied*
  Medium: Concertos (2 pianos); Piano music (2 pianos)
  Year: 1935
  Duration: 20′
  Notes: Also published in *Sochineniia dlia fortepiano*
  First performance: Paris; Salle Gaveau; Igor & Soulima
    Stravinsky, pianos; 21 November 1935
  Contents: (1) Con moto; (2) Notturno; adagietto;
    (3) Quattro variazioni; (4) Prelude e fuga
  Published: (1) B. Schott's Söhne, 1936 (Edition Schott,
    2520) plate no. BSS 34650; (2) Associated Music
    Publishers, 1936 (Edition Schott, 2520)

C39 *Concerto, string orchestra, D*
  Medium: String-orchestra music; Concertos (String
    orchestra)
  Year: 1946
  Alternate title: *Basle concerto*
  Duration: 12′
  Dedication: Basler Kammerorchester & Paul Sacher
  First performance: Basle; Basler Kammerorchester;
    Paul Sacher, conductor; 27 January 1947
  Contents: (1) Vivace; (2) Arioso; andantino; (3) Rondo;
    allegro

Published: (1) Boosey & Hawkes, 1947 (Hawkes pocket
scores, 626) plate no. B&H 16125, LC 65-41855/M;
(2) Muzyka, 1971, in *Kamernye ansambli* (W1)

C40 *Concerto, string orchestra, D (revised)*
Medium: Concertos (String orchestra); String-orchestra
music
Year: 1946 ca.
Published: (1) Boosey & Hawkes, 1961, LC 78-238806

C41 *Concerto, violin, D major*
Medium: Concertos (Violin); Violin with orchestra
Year: 1931
Duration: 22'
Commission: Blair Fairchild
Notes: Violin part written in collaboration with
Samuel Dushkin
First performance: Berlin; Funkorchester; Samuel Dushkin,
violin; Igor Stravinsky, conductor; 23 October 1931
Contents: (1) Toccata; (2) Aria I; (3) Aria II; (4) Capriccio
Published: (1) B. Schott's Söhne, 1931 (Edition Schott,
3504) plate no. BSS 33103; (2) Associated Music
Publishers, 1959, 1931 (Edition Schott, 3504) plate no.
33109; (3) B. Schott's Söhne, 1969, 1959, 1931
(Edition Schott, 49) plate no. BSS 33000, full score,
LC 75-239202

C42 *Concerto, violin, D major; violin & piano*
Medium: Violin and piano music
Notes: Reduction by the composer and Samuel Dushkin
Published: (1) B. Schott's Söhne, 1931 (Edition Schott,
2190) plate no. BSS 32956; (2) Associated Music
Publishers, 1959, 1931 (Edition Schott, 2190);
(3) Muzyka, 1966, ed. David Oistrakh, LC 67-33159/M

C43 *Credo*
  Medium: Choruses (Mixed voices), Unaccompanied
  Year: 1932
  Alternate title: *Simvol viery*
  Duration: 3'
  Notes: Text in Slavonic
  Published: (1) Edition Russe de Musique, 1933, plate no.
    RMV 562; (2) Boosey & Hawkes, 1957

C44 *Credo (1949)*
  Medium: Choruses (Mixed voices), Unaccompanied
  Year: 1949
  Notes: Text in Latin
  Published: (1) Boosey & Hawkes, 1957

C45 *Credo (1964)*
  Medium: Choruses (Mixed voices), Unaccompanied
  Year: 1964
  Notes: Text in Slavonic; erroneously cited as second of
    Three sacred choruses in Boosey & Hawkes *Newsletter*
    (v.2 n.1, Spring 1967)
  Published: (1) Boosey & Hawkes, 1966, plate no. B&H
    19285, LC 66-97493/M

Dance of the princesses
  see *L'oiseau de feu. La ronde des princesses* (O24-O32)

Danse de la ballerine
  see *Petroushka. Danse de la ballerine; arr., women's voices,
    violin & piano* (P21)

Danse des cochers
  see *Petroushka. Danse des cochers et des palefreniers;
    arr., women's voices & piano* (P22)

Danse russe
  see *Petroushka. Danse russe* (P23-P27)

Danse sacrale
see *Le sacre du printemps. Danse sacrale (1943)* (S6)

D1 *Danses concertantes, chamber orchestra*
Medium: Chamber-orchestra music
Year: 1942
Duration: 20′
Commission: Werner Janssen Orchestra of Los Angeles
First performance: Los Angeles; Werner Janssen Orchestra
of Los Angeles; Igor Stravinsky, conductor;
8 February 1942
Contents: (1) Marche; introduction; (2) Pas d'action;
(3) Thème varié; (4) Pas de deux; risoluto; (5) Marche;
conclusion
Published: (1) B. Schott's Söhne, 1952, 1942 (Edition Schott,
4275; Musik des 20. Jahrhunderts) plate no. BSS
38095a; (2) Associated Music Publishers, 1942 (Edition
Schott, 4275) plate no. AS 194238, LC 44-33524

D2 *Danses concertantes, chamber orchestra; arr., 2 pianos*
Medium: Piano music (2 pianos)
Notes: Arranged by Ingolf Dahl
Published: (1) Associated Music Publishers, 1944,
plate no. AS 19439, LC 45-15194

D3 *Dialogue between reason and joy*
Year: 1917
Notes: Unfinished and unpublished

Dievich'i piesni
see *Mavra. Drug moĭ milyĭ; voice & piano* (M7)

Divertimento
see *Le baiser de la fée (Suite)* (B7-B9)

D4 *Double canon, string quartet*
   Medium: String quartets
   Year: 1959
   Alternate title: *Raoul Dufy in memoriam*
   Duration: 1'16"
   First performance: New York; 10 January 1960
   Published: (1) Boosey & Hawkes, 1960, LC M60-1555

D5 *The dove descending breaks the air*
   Medium: Choruses (Mixed voices), Unaccompanied
   Poet: T. S. Eliot
   Year: 1962
   Alternate title: *Anthem*
   Duration: 2'10"
   First performance: Los Angeles; Robert Craft, conductor;
      10 February 1962
   Published: (1) Boosey & Hawkes, 1962, LC 62-39371/M

   Drug moĭ milyĭ
   see entries for *Mavra* (M5-M7)

D6 *Duet, bassoons*
   Medium: Bassoon music (2 bassoons)
   Year: 1918

   Dumbarton Oaks
   see *Concerto, chamber orchestra, E flat* (C32)

D7 *Duo concertante, violin & piano*
   Medium: Violin and piano music
   Year: 1932
   Duration: 16'
   First performance: Berlin; Funkhaus; Igor Stravinsky,
      piano; Samuel Dushkin, violin; 28 October 1932
   Contents: (1) Cantilène; (2) Ecologue I; (3) Ecologue II;
      (4) Gigue; (5) Dithyrambe

Published: (1) Edition Russe de Musique, 1933, plate no.
RMV 564, LC M61-2201; (2) Edition Russe de
Musique, 1938

Dve suity
see *Suite, orchestra. nos. 1 & 2* (S29)

Easy pieces, piano, 4 hands (1917)
see *Pièces faciles, piano, 4 hands (1917)* (P41)

E1 *Ebony concerto, clarinet & jazz ensemble*
Medium: Concertos (Clarinet); Clarinet with jazz ensemble
Year: 1945
Duration: 11'
Dedication: Woody Herman
First performance: New York: Woody Herman, clarinet;
Walter Hendl, conductor; 25 March 1946
Contents: (1) Allegro moderato; (2) Andante; (3) Moderato;
con moto
Published: (1) Charling Music Corporation, Mayfair Music
Corporation, 1946, LC 65-41858rev/M; (2) Edwin H.
Morris, 1954; (3) Charles Hansen Music & Books,
n.d., plate no. E 6156a

E2 *Ebony concerto, clarinet & jazz ensemble; arr.,*
clarinet & band
Medium: Concertos (Clarinet); Clarinet with band
Notes: Arranged by Robert E. Nelson
Published: (1) Edwin H. Morris, 1968, plate no. Ebony
concerto 39; (2) Charles Hansen Music & Books,
n.d., plate no. E 6153

E3 *Elegie, viola, unaccompanied*
Medium: Viola music; Violin music
Year: 1944
Duration: 4'30"

Notes: May be performed on viola or violin
Commission: German Prévost
Dedication: In memoriam Alphonse Onnou
Published: (1) Chappell, Associated Music Publishers,
  1945, plate no. AC 19454; (2) B. Schott's Söhne, 1953
  (Edition Schott, 4477) plate no. BSS 38483

E4 *Elegie, viola, unaccompanied; 2 violas*
  Medium: Viola music (2 violas)

E5 *Elegy for J. F. K.*
  Medium: Songs (Medium voice) with 3 clarinets
  Poet: Wystan Hugh Auden
  Year: 1964
  Dedication: John Fitzgerald Kennedy
  First performance: Los Angeles; Robert Craft, conductor;
    6 April 1964
  Published: (1) Boosey & Hawkes, 1964, plate no. B&H
    19266, for mezzo-soprano; LC 65-45741/M; (2) Boosey
    & Hawkes, 1964, plate no. B&H 19270, for mezzo-
    soprano or baritone, LC 65-45740/M; (3) Boosey &
    Hawkes, 1964, for baritone, LC 65-45721/M

E6 *Epitaphium*
  Medium: Trios (Flute, clarinet, harp)
  Year: 1959
  Alternate title: *Für das Grabmal des Prinzen Max Egon
    zu Fürstenberg*
  Duration: 1'16"
  Dedication: In memoriam Prince Max Egon zu Fürstenberg
  First performance: Donaueschingen; 17 October 1959
  Published: (1) Boosey & Hawkes, 1959, plate no.
    B&H 18599

Etude, piano
see also *Etudes, orchestra. No. 4: Madrid; arr.,*
   2 pianos (E11)

E7 *Etude, piano*
Medium: Piano music
Year: 1917
Alternate title: *Study, piano*
Duration: 2'15"
Notes: Also arranged for 2 pianos as *Madrid* (*see* E11)
   and for orchestra as final movement of *Etudes for
   orchestra* (*see* E8)
Dedication: Eugenia Errazuriz
First performance: London; Aeolian Hall;
   13 October 1921

E8 *Etudes, orchestra*
Medium: Orchestral music
Year: 1928
Alternate title: *Studies, orchestra*
Duration: 12'
Notes: No. 4 arranged from *Etude* for piano (*see* E7);
   absorbed first movement of *Pièces* for string quartet
   (*see* P35)
First performance: Berlin; 7 November 1930
Contents: (1) Danse; (2) Eccentric; (3) Cantique;
   (4) Madrid
Published: (1) Edition Russe de Musique, 1930;
   (2) Boosey & Hawkes, 1947 (Hawkes pocket scores,
   631) plate no. B&H 16309

E9 *Etudes, orchestra (1952)*
Medium: Orchestral music
Year: 1952
Published: (1) Boosey & Hawkes, 1971, LC 72-202416

E10 *Etudes, orchestra. No. 3: Cantique; arr., organ*
     Medium: Organ music
     Notes: Arranged by John Stott; based on final movement
       of *Pièces* for string quartet (*see* P35)
     Published: (1) Boosey & Hawkes, 1968 (Music for organ)
       plate no. B&H 19611, LC 79-207193

E11 *Etudes, orchestra. No. 4: Madrid; arr., 2 pianos*
     Medium: Piano music (2 pianos)
     Alternate title: *Etude for piano* (original title)
     Notes: Arranged by Soulima Stravinsky
     Published: (1) Boosey & Hawkes, 1951, plate no. B&H
       17006, LC 52-30917

E12 *Etudes, piano, op. 7*
     Medium: Piano music
     Year: 1908
     Alternate title: *Studies, piano*
     Dedication: E. Mitusov, Nicholas Richter, Andrei
       Rimsky-Korsakov, Vladimir Rimsky-Korsakov
     Contents: (1) Con moto; (2) Allegro brillante;
       (3) Andantino; (4) Vivo
     Published: (1) Jurgenson, 1910, plate no. 33866-33869,
       LC M61-2321; (2) Anton J. Benjamin, 1925 (Elite
       ed. 3015-3016, Neu-Russische Musiker 3017-3018)
       plate no. AJB 82585-82587, 82589; (3) Associated Music
       Publishers, 1925 (Elite ed., 3015-3018); (4) Inter-
       national Music Co., 1953

E13 *Etudes, piano, op. 7. No. 4: F sharp minor*
     Medium: Piano music
     Published: (1) Marks Corporation, 1936, plate no.
       10342-6, ed. Max Hirschfeld

The fairy's kiss
see *Le baiser de la fée* (B3)

F1 *Fanfare for a new theatre*
Medium: Trumpet music (2 trumpets)
Year: 1964
Dedication: Lincoln Kirstein, George Balanchine
First performance: New York; New York State Theater;
19 April 1964
Published: (1) Boosey & Hawkes, 1968, plate no. 19650,
LC 68-44635/M

Faun and shepherdess
see *Le faune et la bergère, op. 2* (F2)

Faun und Schäferin
see *Le faune et la bergère, op. 2* (F2)

F2 *Le faune et la bergère, op. 2*
Medium: Songs (Medium voice) with orchestra
Poet: A. Pushkin
Year: 1906
Alternate title: (1) *Faun and shepherdess*; (2) *Faun und Schäferin*; (3) *Favny i pastushka*
Duration: 10'
Notes: French translation by A. Komaroff; German translation by Heinrich Möller
Dedication: Ekaterina Gabrielovna Stravinsky
First performance: St. Petersburg; Russian Symphony Orchestra; Felix Blumenfeld, conductor;
16 February 1905
Contents: (1) La bergère (Shepherdess; Pastushka);
andantino; (2) Le faune (Faun; Favny); allegro moderato;
(3) Le torrent (Torrent; Rieka); andante; allegro
Published: (1) M. P. Belaieff, 1964, 1913, plate no. 2925;
(2) Boosey & Hawkes

F3 *Le faune et la bergère; voice & piano*
Medium: Songs (Medium voice) with piano
Published: (1) M. P. Belaieff, 1927, 1908, plate no. 2800

Favny i pastushka
see *Le faune et la bergère, op. 2* (F2)

Fête populaire de la semaine grasse
see *Petroushka. Fête populaire de la semaine grasse* (P28)

F4 *Feu d'artifice, op. 4*
Medium: Orchestral music
Year: 1908
Alternate title: (1) *Feuerwerk*; (2) *Fireworks*
Duration: 4'
Dedication: Nadia and Maximilian Steinberg
First performance: St. Petersburg; Alexandre Siloti,
conductor; 6 February 1909
Published: (1) B. Schott's Söhne, 1910, plate no. 28616,
LC 61-2092; (2) B. Schott's Söhne, 194?, 1922
(Edition Schott, 3464) plate no. BSS 28616a, LC 61-2075;
(3) Associated Music Publishers, n.d. (Edition Schott,
3464); (4) International Music Co., 1948, LC 50-15340

F5 *Feu d'artifice, op. 4; piano*
Medium: Piano music

F6 *Feu d'artifice, op. 4; arr., piano, 4 hands*
Medium: Piano music (4 hands)
Notes: Arranged by Otto Singer
Published: (1) B. Schott's Söhne, 1924 (Edition Schott,
962) plate no. BSS 31157

Feuerwerk
see *Feu d'artifice, op. 4* (F4)

The firebird
see *L'oiseau de feu* (O8)

Fireworks
see *Feu d'artifice, op. 4* (F4)

Flohlied
see Z2

F7 *The flood*
Medium: Operas
Year: 1962
Alternate title: *Noah and the ark*
Duration: 24'
First performance: CBS television, 14 June 1962
Published: (1) Boosey & Hawkes, 1963 (Hawkes pocket
scores, 746) LC 63-39578/M

F8 *The flood. Piano-vocal score*
Medium: Piano-vocal scores
Published: (1) Boosey & Hawkes, 1963, 1962,
LC 63-34555/M

The fox
see *Renard* (R7)

Für das Grabmal des Prinzen Max Egon zu Fürstenberg
see *Epitaphium* (E6)

Funeral dirge
see *Chant funèbre sur la morte de Rimsky-Korsakov,
op. 5* (C17)

Gavotte con variazioni
see *Pulcinella. Gavotte con variazioni; piano* (P64)

Un grand sommeil noir
see *Poèmes de Verlaine, op. 9* (P45)

G1 *Greeting prelude, orchestra*
   Medium: Orchestral music
   Year: 1955
   Duration: 45″
   Dedication: Pierre Monteux
   First performance: Boston Symphony Orchestra;
      Charles Munch, conductor; 4 April 1955
   Published: (1) Boosey & Hawkes, 1956, LC M56-1694

H1 *L'histoire du soldat*
   Medium: Melodramas with instrumental septet
   Poet: C. F. Ramuz
   Year: 1918
   Alternate title: *The soldier's tale*
   Duration: 35′
   Notes: English translation by Rosa Newmarch, and also by
      Michael Flanders and Kitty Black; German translation
      by Hans Reinhart
   Dedication: Werner Reinhart
   First performance: Lausanne; Ernest Ansermet, conductor;
      28 September 1918

   Contents: (1) The soldier's march; marching tunes;
      (2) Airs by a stream; (3) The soldier's march; marching
      tunes; (4) Pastorale; (5) Pastorale; (6) Airs by a stream;
      (7) The soldier's march; marching tunes; (8) Royal
      march; (9) The little concert; (10) Three dances:
      tango, waltz, ragtime; (11) The devil's dance;
      (12) The little chorale; (13) The devil's song; (14) The
      great chorale; (15) The devil's triumphal march
   Published: (1) J. & W. Chester, 1924, plate no. W.Ph.V. 294
      J.W.C. 44b; (2) International Music Co., 196?,
      LC M60-2700; (3) Edwin F. Kalmus, n.d.

H2   *L'histoire du soldat. Libretto*
Medium: Librettos
Published: (1) Edwin F. Kalmus, n.d., text in English

H3   *L'histoire du soldat. Piano-vocal score*
Medium: Piano-vocal scores
Published: (1) J. & W. Chester, 1924, plate no. 9712,
   LC M61-2202

H4   *L'histoire du soldat (Suite)*
Medium: Septets
First performance: London; Ernest Ansermet, conductor;
   20 July 1920
Contents: (1) The soldier's march; marching tunes;
   (2) Airs by a stream; (3) Royal march; (4) The little
   concert; (5) Three dances: tango, waltz, ragtime;
   (6) The devil's dance; (7) The great chorale; (8) The
   devil's triumphal march
Published: (1) J. & W. Chester, 1922

H5   *L'histoire du soldat (Suite); piano, clarinet & violin*
Medium: Trios (Piano, clarinet, violin)
Year: 1919
Duration: 25'
First performance: Lausanne; 8 November 1919
Contents: (1) The soldier's march; marching tunes;
   (2) Airs by a stream; (3) The little concert; (4) Three
   dances: tango, waltz, ragtime; (5) The devil's dance
Published: (1) J. & W. Chester, 1920 (Chester library)
   plate no. JWC 222; (2) International Music Co., 196?,
   plate no. 1548, LC M60-2862

H6   *L'histoire du soldat. Devil's dance; arr., piano*
Medium: Piano music

Notes: Arranged by Gregory Stone
Published: (1) Marks Music Corporation, 1941
  (Kaleidoscope edition, 11504); (2) Marks Music Corpo-
  ration, 1936 (Album of Igor Stravinsky masterpieces;
  Contemporary masterpieces, n. 9)

H7 *L'histoire du soldat. Valse; arr., piano*
  Medium: Piano music
  Published: (1) J. & W. Chester

H8 *Histoires pour enfants*
  Medium: Songs (Medium voice) with piano
  Poet: After popular Russian texts
  Year: 1917
  Alternate title: *Tales for children*
  Duration: 2′
  Notes: Nos. 1 and 2 also used in his *Songs* (see S25)
    as nos. 4 and 3; French translation by C. F. Ramuz
  Dedication: "Pour mon fils cadet"
  Contents: (1) Tilimbom (Tilim-bom); (2) Les canards,
    les cynges, les oies (Gusilebedi); (3) Chanson de l'ours
    (Piesenka medviedia)
  Published: (1) J. & W. Chester, 1920, LC 76-217051;
    (2) J. & W. Chester, 1927, plate no. 3830

H9 *Histoires pour enfants; piano*
  Medium: Piano music

H10 *Histoires pour enfants. No. 1: Tilimbom; voice & orchestra*
  Medium: Songs with orchestra
  Year: 1923
  Published: (1) B. Schott's Söhne

  Hymne à la nouvelle Russie
  see Z5

I1 *In memoriam Dylan Thomas*
  Medium: Songs (High voice) with string quartet
    and 4 trombones
  Year: 1954
  Duration: 6′
  First performance: Los Angeles; Robert Craft, conductor;
    20 September 1954
  Published: (1) Boosey & Hawkes, 1954 (Hawkes pocket
    scores, 688) plate no. B&H 17597, LC M54-2701;
    (2) Boosey & Hawkes, 1954, full score

I2 *In memoriam Dylan Thomas; voice & piano*
  Medium: Songs with piano
  Year: 1954
  Published: (1) Boosey & Hawkes, 1954, plate no.
    B&H 17637, LC M57-110

I3 *Instrumental miniatures, winds & strings*
  Medium: Instrumental ensembles
  Year: 1962
  Duration: 8′
  Notes: Based on nos. 1, 7, 6, 3, 5, 2, 4 and 8 of
    Les cinq doigts (see C20)
  Dedication: Laurence Morton
  First performance: Toronto; members of the CBC
    Symphony Orchestra; Igor Stravinsky, conductor;
    29 April 1962
  Contents: (1) Andantino; (2) Vivace; (3) Lento;
    (4) Allegretto; (5) Moderato alla breve; (6) Tempo di
    marcia; (7) Larghetto; (8) Tempo di tango
  Published: (1) J. & W. Chester, 1963, plate no. J.W.C.
    9906A, miniature score, LC 64-38418/M; (2) J. & W.
    Chester, 1962, holograph reproduction, LC 63-34297/M

I4 *Introitus*
  Medium: Choruses (Men's voices) with instrumental
    ensemble
  Year: 1965
  Alternate title: *T. S. Eliot in memoriam*
  Duration: 3'30"
  Dedication: T. S. Eliot
  First performance: Chicago; 17 April 1965
  Published: (1) Boosey & Hawkes, 1965 (Hawkes pocket
    scores, 780) LC 66-45960/M

Izy vospominaniĭ iunasheskikhy
  see *Petites chansons* (P13)

Japanese lyrics
  see *Poésie de la lyrique japonaise* (P51)

Jeu de cartes
  see *The card party* (C11)

Das Kartenspiel
  see *The card party* (C11)

Katzenlieder
  see *Berceuses du chat* (B13)

Khovanshchina
  see Z12

Kobald
  see Z9

König Oedipus
  see *Oedipus rex* (O5)

Lamentationes Jeremiae prophetae
  see *Threni* (T6)

Largo, piano
  see *Concerto, piano & band. Largo; piano* (C37)

Le libertin
see *The rake's progress* (R3)

L1 *Little canon*
Medium: Vocal duets
Poet: Jean de Meung
Year: 1947
Alternate title: (1) *Petite canon pour la fête de Nadia Boulanger*; (2) *Canon, 2 tenors*

Little songs
see *Petites chansons* (P13)

Lullaby
see *The rake's progress. Lullaby; 2 recorders* (R6)

Madrid
see *Etudes, orchestra. No. 4: Madrid; arr., 2 pianos* (E11)

March
see *Pièces faciles, piano, 4 hands (1915). No. 1: March; instrumental ensemble* (P37)

Marche chinoise
see *Le chant du rossignol. Marche chinoise; arr., piano* (C15) and *Le rossignol* (R13)

La marseillaise
see Z10

M1 *Mass*
Medium: Choruses (Mixed voices) with winds
Year: 1948
Duration: 17'
First performance: Milano; Teatro alla Scala; Ernest Ansermet, conductor; 27 October 1948
Contents: (1) Kyrie; (2) Gloria; (3) Credo; (4) Sanctus; (5) Agnus Dei

Published: (1) Boosey & Hawkes, 1948, plate no. B&H
16501, LC 49-12718rev; (2) Boosey & Hawkes,
1948 (Hawkes pocket scores, 655) plate no. B&H 16501,
LC 49-12718rev

M2 *Mass. Piano-vocal score*
Medium: Piano-vocal scores
Notes: Arranged by Leopold Spinner
Published: (1) Boosey & Hawkes, 1948, plate no. B&H
16403, LC 49-14898

M3 *Mavra*
Medium: Operas
Poet: Boris Kochno, after A. Pushkin
Year: 1922
Duration: 25'
Notes: English translation by Robert Burness, also by
Robert Craft; French translation by Jacques Larmanjat;
German translation by A. Elukhen
Dedication: In memoriam Pushkin, Glinka and
Tschaikowsky
First performance: Paris; Ballet Russe; Gregor Fitelberg,
conductor; 3 June 1925
Contents: (1) Overture; (2) Parasha's song; (3) Hussar's
gypsy song; (4) Dialogue; (5) The mother's song;
(6) Dialogue; (7) Duet; (8) Dialogue; (9) Quartet;
(10) Dialogue; (11) Duet; (12) Dialogue; (13) Mavra's
song; (14) Coda
Published: (1) Edition Russe de Musique, 1925, plate no.
RMV 418; (2) Boosey & Hawkes, 1956, LC M57-880;
(3) Boosey & Hawkes, 1956 (Hawkes pocket scores,
843); (4) Boosey & Hawkes, 1969, English translation
by Robert Craft, LC 70-223629

M4 *Mavra. Piano-vocal score*
Medium: Piano-vocal score
Notes: Reduction by the composer and Albert Spaulding
Published: (1) Edition Russe de Musique, 1925,
    text in English, French, German and Russian,
    LC M61-2187; (2) Boosey & Hawkes, 1947, plate no.
    B&H 16304, in English, French and German; (3) Boosey &
    Hawkes, Edition Russe de Musique, 1956, LC M57-880

M5 *Mavra. Drug moĭ milyĭ; violin & piano*
Medium: Violin and piano music
Year: 1937
Alternate title: (1) *Chanson russe*; (2) *Russian maiden's
    song*; (3) *Chanson de Parasha*
Notes: Arranged by the composer and Samuel Dushkin
Published: (1) Edition Russe de Musique, 1938; (2) Boosey
    & Hawkes, 1947, plate no. 17860; (3) Boosey & Hawkes,
    1948 LC 49-15671rev

M6 *Mavra. Drug moĭ milyĭ; violoncello & piano*
Medium: Violoncello and piano music
Notes: Arranged by the composer and Dmitri Markevitch
Published: (1) Edition Russe de Musique; (2) Boosey
    & Hawkes, 1951, plate no. 17815

M7 *Mavra. Drug moĭ milyĭ; voice & piano*
Medium: Songs with piano
Year: 1947
Alternate title: (1) *Russian maiden's song*; (2) *Chanson
    russe*; (3) *Chanson de Parasha*; (4) *Dievich'i piesni*
Published: (1) Edition Russe de Musique, 1925, based on
    piano-vocal score; (2) Boosey & Hawkes, 1948,
    English translation by Robert Burness, with Russian
    text, LC 48-15671rev

M8 *Mavra. Net' ne zabyt'; voice & piano*
   Medium: Songs with piano
   Alternate title: (1) *Chanson de la mère*; (2) *Mother's song*
   Published: (1) Boosey & Hawkes,

M9 *Mavra. Overture; piano*
   Medium: Piano music
   Published: (1) Boosey & Hawkes,

M10 *Mavra. Selections; arr., jazz ensemble*
   Medium: Jazz ensembles
   Notes: Arranged by Jack Hylton
   First performance: Paris; Jack Hylton, conductor; ca. 1932
   Contents: (1) Duet; (2) Quartet

M11 *Mélodies, op. 6*
   Medium: Songs (Medium voice) with piano
   Poet: S. Gorodetzky
   Year: 1908
   Duration: 8'
   Notes: German translation by S. Gorodetzky; French
      and English translations by M. D. Calvocoressi
   First performance: St. Petersburg; Elizabeth Petrenko,
      soprano; Igor Stravinsky, piano; 1908
   Contents: (1) Chanson de printemps: la novice (Spring:
      the cloister; Vesna: monastyirskaia); (2) La rosée sainte:
      chant mystique des vieux-croyants flagellants (A song
      of the ancient Russian flagellants; Rosianka:
      Khlistovskaia)
   Published: (1) Jurgenson, 1912 or 1913, plate no. 3364-5

M12 *Monumentum pro Gesualdo de Venosa ad CD annum*
   Medium: Orchestral music
   Year: 1960

Duration: 7'

Notes: Based on madrigals of Gesualdo (Libro 5, n. 14;
   Libro 5, n. 18; Libro 6, n. 2)

First performance: Venezia; Orchestra del Teatro la Fenice;
   Igor Stravinsky, conductor; 27 September 1960

Contents: (1) Asciugate i begli occhi; (2) Ma tu, cagion
   di quella; (3) Beltà poi che t'assenti

Published: (1) Boosey & Hawkes, 1960 (Hawkes pocket
   scores, 725) plate no. 18748, LC M60-2846; (2) Boosey
   & Hawkes, 1960, full score

Mother's song
   see *Mavra. Net' ne zabyt'; voice & piano* (M8)

M13 *Movements, piano & orchestra*
   Medium: Piano with orchestra
   Year: 1959
   Notes: Also published in *Sochineniia dlia fortepiano*
      (*see* W2)
   Dedication: Margrit Weber
   First performance: New York; Margrit Weber, piano;
      Igor Stravinsky, conductor; 10 January 1960
   Contents: Five movements with tempo indications given by
      metronome markings
   Published: (1) Boosey & Hawkes, 1960 (Hawkes pocket
      scores, 718) plate no. B&H 18676; (2) Boosey & Hawkes,
      1960, full score, LC M60-2170

M14 *Movements, piano & orchestra; 2 pianos*
   Medium: Piano music (2 pianos)
   Year: 1959
   Published: (1) Boosey & Hawkes, 1960, plate no.
      B&H 18647, LC M60-2169

M15 *The mushrooms going to war*
  Medium: Songs (Low voice) with piano
  Year: 1904

 Die Nachtigall
   see *Le rossignol* (R13)

 Net' ne zabyt'
   see *Mavra. Net' ne zabyt'; voice & piano* (M8)

 The nightingale
   see *Le rossignol* (R13)

 Noah and the ark
   see *The flood* (F7)

N1 *Les noces*
  Medium: Ballets; Choruses (Mixed voices) with
    instrumental ensemble
  Poet: Stravinsky, after popular Russian texts collected by
    Afanasiev and Kireievsky
  Year: 1923
  Alternate titles: (1) *The wedding*; (2) *Svadebka*
  Duration: 35'
  Notes: Orchestrated in 1923, although composed in 1917;
    French translation by C. F. Ramuz; English translation
    by D. Millar Craig
  Dedication: Serge Diaghilev
  First performance: Paris; Ballet Russe; Ernest Ansermet,
    conductor; 13 June 1923
  Published: (1) J. & W. Chester, 1923, plate no. JWC 9718,
    full score; (2) J. & W. Chester, 1923, plate no. JWC
    45; (3) J. & W. Chester, 192?, plate no. W.Ph.V.
    JWC 45b, full score

N2 *Les noces. Piano-vocal score*
Medium: Piano-vocal scores
Published: (1) J. & W. Chester, 1922, plate no. J.W.C.
9718, text in French and Russian, LC 63-26470/M

N3 *Norwegian moods*
Medium: Orchestral music
Year: 1942
Alternate title: *Pièces à la norvegiénne*
Duration: 8'30"
First performance: Cambridge, Mass.; Sanders Theater;
Boston Symphony Orchestra; Igor Stravinsky,
conductor; 13 January 1944
Contents: (1) Intrada; (2) Song; (3) Wedding dance;
(4) Cortège
Published: (1) Associated Music Publishers, 1944, plate no.
AS 19449, LC 45-18360rev/M; (2) B. Schott's Söhne,
ca. 1972, 1968, 1944

O1 *Octet, winds*
Medium: Wind octets
Year: 1923
Duration: 16'
Notes: Ed. by Albert Spaulding
Dedication: Vera de Bosset Stravinsky
First performance: Paris; Concerts Koussevitsky; Igor
Stravinsky, conductor; 18 October 1923
Contents: (1) Sinfonia; (2) Tema con variazioni;
(3) Finale
Published: (1) Edition Russe de Musique, 1924, LC
M61-2088; (2) Muzyka, 1971, in *Kamernye
ansambli* (W1)

O2 *Octet, winds (1952)*
Medium: Wind octets
Year: 1952
Published: (1) Boosey & Hawkes, 1952 (Hawkes pocket
    scores, 630) plate no. B&H 17231, LC M53-871;
    (2) Boosey & Hawkes, 1952, full score

O3 *Octet, winds; arr., piano*
Medium: Piano music
Notes: Arranged by Arthur Lourié
Published: (1) Edition Russe de Musique, 1926, plate no.
    RMV 421, LC M61-2203; (2) Boosey & Hawkes,
    1952, plate no. B&H 17270

O4 *Ode, orchestra*
Medium: Orchestral music
Year: 1943
Duration: 11'
Commission: Serge Koussevitsky
Dedication: In memoriam Natalie Koussevitsky
First performance: Boston; Boston Symphony Orchestra;
    Serge Koussevitsky, conductor; 8 October 1943
Contents: (1) Eulogy; lento; (2) Ecologue; con moto;
    (3) Epitaph; lento
Published: (1) B. Schott's Söhne, 1947, LC M55-2158;
    (2) Associated Music Publishers, 1947, plate no. AMP
    194551, LC M55-2158; (3) B. Schott's Söhne, 1969, 1947
    (Musik des 20. Jahrhunderts; Edition Schott, 5942)
    plate no. BSS 42319, LC 70-270898

O5 *Oedipus rex*
Medium: Operas; Oratorios
Poet: Igor Stravinsky and Jean Cocteau, with Latin transla-
    tion by J. Daniélou, German translation by L. Thurneiser

Year: 1927

First performance: Paris; Théâtre Sarah Bernhardt; Ballet
Russe; Igor Stravinsky, conductor; 30 May 1927

Published: (1) Edition Russe de Musique, 1928,
LC 51-48027

O6 *Oedipus rex (1948)*

Medium: Operas; Oratorios

Year: 1948

Notes: English translation by E. E. Cummings

Published: (1) Boosey & Hawkes, 1949 (Hawkes pocket
scores, 651) plate no. B&H 16497, LC 49-28996

O7 *Oedipus rex. Piano-vocal score*

Medium: Piano-vocal scores

Published: (1) Boosey & Hawkes, 1950, LC 62-37350/M;
(2) Boosey & Hawkes, 1949, plate no. 16992; (3) Edition
Russe de Musique, 1948, 1928, 1926, plate no. RMV 431

O8 *L'oiseau de feu*

Medium: Ballets; Orchestral music

Year: 1910

Alternate titles: (1) *The firebird*; (2) *Zhar-ptitsa*

Duration: 40'

Notes: Music of finale also used for *Canon on a Russian
popular theme* (C1)

Commission: Serge Diaghilev

Dedication: Andrei Rimsky-Korsakov

First performance: Paris; Ballet Russe; Gabriel Pierné,
conductor; 25 June 1910

Published: (1) Jurgenson, 1910, plate no. 34920;
(2) Broude Brothers, 195?, plate no. BB 50, LC M53-16;
(3) Gosudarstvennyi Muzykal'noe izd-vo, 1964,
LC 64-52535M; (4) B. Schott's Söhne, 1973
(Edition Schott, 6461)

O9 *L'oiseau de feu; piano*
   Medium: Piano music
   Year: 1910
   Published: (1) B. Schott's Söhne, 1936 (Edition Schott,
      3279) plate no. BSS 34726; (2) Jurgenson, 1910,
      plate no. 34903-34919, LC 76-231869

O10 *L'oiseau de feu (Suite)*
   Medium: Orchestral music
   Year: 1911
   Duration: 21'
   Contents: (1) Introduction; (2) Supplication; (3) Jeux
      des princesses; (4) La ronde des princesses;
      (5) Danse infernale
   Published: (1) Jurgenson, 1913, plate no. 35965,
      printed from plates for ballet

O11 *L'oiseau de feu (Suite, 1919)*
   Medium: Orchestral music
   Year: 1919
   Duration: 26'
   Contents: (1) Introduction; (2) L'oiseau de feu et sa danse;
      (3) Ronde de princesses; (4) Danse infernale du roi
      Kastcheï; (5) Berceuse; (6) Finale
   Published: (1) J. & W. Chester, 1923, 1920 (Edition Schott,
      3467) plate no. JWC 17, LC 44-21555; (2) Edwin F.
      Kalmus, n.d. (E. F. Kalmus orchestral score, 41);
      (3) Boosey & Hawkes, n.d. (Hawkes pocket scores, 573)

O12 *L'oiseau de feu (Suite, 1945)*
   Medium: Orchestral music
   Year: 1945
   Duration: 28'

Contents: (1) Introduction; (2) Prelude and dance;
(3) Variations; (4) Pantomime I; (5) Pas de deux;
(6) Pantomime II; (7) Scherzo; (8) Pantomime III;
(9) Infernal dance; (10) Lullaby; (11) Final hymn
Published: (1) Leeds Music Corporation, 1946; (2) Leeds
Music Corporation, 1947; (3) B. Schott's Söhne, 1947
(Edition Schott, 4420) plate no. BSS 38597a; (4) Broude
Brothers, 195?, plate no. BB 50, LC M53-16; (5) B.
Schott's Söhne, 1954 (Edition Schott, 73) plate no.
BSS 38597, full score

O13 *L'oiseau de feu. Berceuse (revised)*
Medium: Orchestral music
Notes: Orchestrated for fewer wind instruments
Published: (1) Jurgenson, 1912; (2) B. Schott's Söhne

O14 *L'oiseau de feu. Berceuse; violin & piano*
Medium: Violin and piano music
Year: 1929
Duration: 3'30"
Dedication: Paul Kochanski
Published: (1) B. Schott's Söhne, 1929 (Edition Schott,
2081) plate no. BSS 32374; (2) Associated Music
Publishers, n.d. (Edition Schott, 2081)

O15 *L'oiseau de feu. Berceuse; violin & piano (1932)*
Medium: Violin and piano music
Year: 1932
Duration: 3'30"
Notes: Arranged by the composer and Samuel Dushkin
Published: (1) B. Schott's Söhne, 1932 (Edition Schott,
2186) plate no. BSS 33324, LC 66-88623; (2) Associated
Music Publishers, 1932 (Edition Schott, 2186)

O16 *L'oiseau de feu. Berceuse; arr., band*
   Medium: Band music
   Notes: Arranged by Maurice Gardner
   Published: (1) Staff Music Publishing Co., 1955

O17 *L'oiseau de feu. Berceuse; arr., bassoon & piano*
   Medium: Bassoon and piano music
   Notes: Arranged by Quinto Maganini
   Published: (1) Edition Musicus, 1948

O18 *L'oiseau de feu. Berceuse; arr., piano*
   Medium: Piano music
   Duration: 3'30"
   Published: (1) Charles W. Homeyer & Co., 1915, plate no.
   CWH 141-2, arranged by George Copeland; (2) Boston
   Music Co., 1917, plate no. 5550, arranged by Charles
   Roepper; (3) B. Schott's Söhne, 1937 (Edition Schott,
   2547) plate no. BSS 34986, arranged by Franz Willms;
   (4) Associated Music Publishers, 1937 (Edition Schott,
   2547) arranged by Franz Willms

O19 *L'oiseau de feu. Berceuse; arr., string orchestra*
   Medium: String orchestra music
   Notes: Arranged by Quinto Maganini, based on 1919 version
   Published: (1) Edition Musicus, 1940, LC 44-36851

O20 *L'oiseau de feu. Berceuse; arr., violin & piano*
   Medium: Violin and piano music
   Notes: Arranged by Quinto Maganini and Rudolf Forst
   Published: (1) Edition Musicus, 1946

O21 *L'oiseau de feu. Berceuse; arr., violoncello & piano*
   Medium: Violoncello and piano music
   Notes: Arranged by Quinto Maganini
   Published: (1) Edition Musicus, 1948

O22 *L'oiseau de feu. Berceuse; arr., women's voices & piano*
Medium: Choruses (Women's voices) and piano
Poet: Gena Branscomb
Alternate title: *Sleep, sleep*
Published: (1) Galaxy Music, 1937, plate no. GM 762-6

O23 *L'oiseau de feu. Danse infernale; arr., piano*
Medium: Piano music
Notes: Arranged by Frederick Block
Published: (1) Marks Music Corporation, 1941
(Kaleidoscope edition, 11517-12) LC 75-231255

O24 *L'oiseau de feu. La ronde des princesses; piano*
Medium: Piano music
Published: (1) Marks Music Corporation, n.d.
(Kaleidoscope edition, 11534-4ph); (2) Marks Music
Corporation, 1936 (Album of Igor Stravinsky
masterpieces, n.9)

O25 *L'oiseau de feu. La ronde des princesses; arr., oboe,
bassoon & piano*
Medium: Trios (Piano, oboe, bassoon)
Published: (1) Edition Musicus, 1942

O26 *L'oiseau de feu. La ronde des princesses; arr., oboe,
clarinet & piano*
Medium: Trios (Piano, oboe, clarinet)
Published: (1) Edition Musicus, 1942

O27 *L'oiseau de feu. La ronde des princesses; arr., organ*
Medium: Organ music
Published: (1) J. & W. Chester, 1922, plate no. 3032,3,
arranged by Maurice Besly; (2) Organ Music Co.,
Western International Music, 1966, arranged by Brook

P. Piper; (3) H. W. Gray, 1917 (HR series, 2; Historical
recital series for the organ) arranged by Clarence
Dickinson

O28 *L'oiseau de feu. La ronde des princesses; arr., piano*
Medium: Piano music
Duration: 2'30"
Notes: Arranged by Franz Willms
Published: (1) B. Schott's Söhne, Associated Music
Publishers, 1937 (Edition Schott, 2548) plate
no. BSS 34985

O29 *L'oiseau de feu. La ronde des princesses; arr., viola & piano*
Medium: Viola and piano music
Notes: Arranged by Quinto Maganini and Rudolf Forst
Published: (1) Edition Musicus, 1946

O30 *L'oiseau de feu. La ronde des princesses; arr., violin, viola
& piano*
Medium: Trios (Viola, violin & piano)
Published: (1) Edition Musicus, 1942

O31 *L'oiseau de feu. La ronde des princesses; arr., voice & piano*
Medium: Songs with piano
Poet: John Klenner
Alternate title: *Summer moon*
Notes: Arranged by Lou Singer
Published: (1) Leeds Music Corporation, 1948, 1946

O32 *L'oiseau de feu. La ronde des princesses; arr.,
women's voices & piano*
Medium: Choruses (Women's voices) with piano
Notes: Arranged by William Lester
Published: (1) Associated Music Publishers, 1925 (A23);
(2) B. Schott's Söhne

O33 *L'oiseau de feu. Scherzo; violin & piano*
   Medium: Violin and piano music
   Year: 1933
   Duration: 2'30"
   Notes: Arranged by the composer and Samuel Dushkin
   Dedication: Paul Kochanski
   Published: (1) B. Schott's Söhne, 1933 (Edition Schott, 2250) plate no. BSS 33683; (2) Associated Music Publishers, 1933 (Edition Schott, 2250)

O34 *L'oiseau de feu. Selections; violin & piano*
   Medium: Violin and piano music
   Year: 1929
   Duration: 3'30"
   Dedication: Paul Kochanski
   Contents: (1) Prélude; (2) La ronde des princesses

O35 *L'oiseau de feu. Selections; arr., orchestra*
   Medium: Orchestral music
   Published: (1) BMI, 1947, arranged by Maurice Brown; (2) Belwin, 1969 (Belwin orchestra, 2nd series) arranged by Merle J. Isaac, LC 77-223293

O36 *L'oiseau de feu. Selections; arr., organ*
   Medium: Organ music
   Notes: Arranged by Maurice Besly
   Contents: (1) Berceuse; (2) Finale
   Published: (1) J. & W. Chester

O37 *L'oiseau de feu. Selections; arr., piano*
   Medium: Piano music
   Published: (1) B. Schott's Söhne, 1934 (Edition Schott, 2378) plate no. BSS 34118-34120, contains Infernal dance, berceuse and finale, arranged by Guido Agosti;

(2) Marks Music Corporation, 1941 (Kaleidoscope edition, 11516-4) contains Berceuse and finale to tableau 2, arranged by Frederick Block, LC 70-231311; (3) Marks Music Corporation, 1936 (Album of Igor Stravinsky masterpieces; Contemporary masterpieces, n. 9) contains Berceuse and finale to tableau 2, arranged by Frederick Block; (4) Associated Music Publishers, 1934 (Edition Schott, 3279) arranged by Guido Agosti

O38 *L'oiseau de feu. Supplications; arr., piano*
Medium: Piano music
Notes: Arranged by Frederick Block
Published: (1) Marks Music Corporation, 1941 (Kaleidoscope edition, 11514) LC 78-231237; (2) Marks Music Corporation, 1936 (Album of Igor Stravinsky masterpieces; Contemporary masterpieces, n. 9)

O39 *L'oiseau de feu. Supplications; arr., violin & piano*
Medium: Violin and piano music
Published: (1) Marks Music Corporation, 1935 (Edition A. Fassio)

Orphée
see *Orpheus* (O40)

O40 *Orpheus*
Medium: Ballets; Orchestral music
Year: 1947
Alternate title: *Orphée*
Duration: 30'
First performance: New York; Ballet Society; 28 April 1948
Published: (1) Boosey & Hawkes, 1948 (Hawkes pocket scores, 640) plate no. B&H 16285, LC 48-21151; (2) Boosey & Hawkes, 1948, full score; (3) Muzyka, 1972, published with *Agon*

O41 *Orpreus; arr., piano*
  Medium: Piano music
  Notes: Arranged by Leopold Spinner
  Published: (1) Boosey & Hawkes, 1948, plate no. B&H 16502

Otche nashy
  see *Pater noster* (P7)

O42 *The owl and the pussy cat*
  Medium: Songs (Medium voice) with piano
  Text: Edward Lear
  Year: 1966
  Published: (1) Boosey & Hawkes, 1967, LC 66-51534/M

P1 *Pastorale*
  Medium: Vocalises (Medium voice) with piano
  Year: 1907
  Duration: 4'
  Dedication: Nadezhda Rimsky-Korsakov
  First performance: St. Petersburg; Elizabeth Petrenko,
    soprano; Igor Stravinsky, piano; 1908
  Published: (1) Jurgenson, 1910, plate no. 34546; (2) J. & W.
    Chester, 1923; (3) B. Schott's Söhne, 1948 (Edition
    Schott, 2295) plate no. BSS 37191; (4) Associated
    Music Publishers, 1948

P2 *Pastorale; oboe, English horn, clarinet, bassoon & violin*
  Medium: Quintets
  Year: 1933
  Duration: 6'
  Notes: Arranged by the composer and Samuel Dushkin
  Published: (1) B. Schott's Söhne, 1934 (Edition Schott,
    3313) plate no. BSS 33967a; (2) Associated Music
    Publishers, 1934

P3 *Pastorale; soprano, oboe, English horn, clarinet, bassoon*
  Medium: Vocalises (Medium voice) with instrumental
    ensemble
  Year: 1923
  Published: (1) Robert Forberg, n.d.?; (2) B. Schott's Söhne,
    1929 (Edition Schott, 3399) plate no. BSS 32375

P4 *Pastorale; violin & piano*
  Medium: Violin and piano music
  Year: 1933
  Duration: 6'
  Notes: Arranged by the composer and Samuel Dushkin
  Published: (1) B. Schott's Söhne, 1934 (Edition Schott,
    2294) plate no. BSS 33976; (2) Associated Music
    Publishers, 1934; (3) Gosudarstvennyi Muzykal'noe,
    1963

P5 *Pastorale; arr., flute & piano*
  Medium: Flute and piano music
  Notes: Arranged by Quinto Maganini
  Published: Edition Musicus, 1942, plate no. 345

P6 *Pastorale; arr., piano*
  Medium: Piano music
  Notes: Arranged by Frederick Block
  Published: (1) Marks Music Corporation, 1941

P7 *Pater noster*
  Medium: Choruses (Mixed voices), Unaccompanied
  Year: 1926
  Alternate title: *Otche nashy*
  Duration: 1'10"
  Notes: Text in Slavonic
  Published: (1) Edition Russe de Musique, 1932, plate no.
    RMV 545; (2) Boosey & Hawkes, 1969

P8 *Pater noster (1949)*
> Medium: Choruses (Mixed voices), Unaccompanied
> Year: 1949
> Notes: Text in Latin
> Published: (1) Boosey & Hawkes, 1949, plate no. 1833

P9 *Perséphone*
> Medium: Choruses (Mixed voices) with orchestra; Ballets
> Poet: André Gide
> Year: 1934
> Duration: 45'
> First performance: Paris; Opéra; Ballet Ida Rubenstein;
>   Igor Stravinsky, conductor; 30 April 1934
> Published: (1) Edition Russe de Musique, 1934;
>   (2) Boosey & Hawkes, full score

P10 *Perséphone (1949)*
> Medium: Choruses (Mixed voices) with orchestra; Ballets
> Year: 1949
> Published: (1) Boosey & Hawkes, Edition Russe de Musique
>   (Hawkes pocket scores) plate no. B&H 16459,
>   LC 51-25136

P11 *Perséphone. Piano-vocal score*
> Medium: Piano-vocal scores
> Notes: Reduction by Sviatoslav Stravinsky in 1934
> Published: (1) Edition Russe de Musique, 1934, plate no.
>   RMV 581; (2) Boosey & Hawkes, 1957, plate no.
>   B&H 16302

Pesante
> see *Le cinq doigts. No. 8: Pesante; instrumental
>   ensemble* (C22)

Pesnia o blokhe
> see Z13

P'esny i kontsertino
    see *Pièces, string quartet* (P35)

Petit canon pour la fête de Nadia Boulanger
    see *Little canon* (L1)

P12 *Petit ramusianum harmonique*
    Medium: Songs, Unaccompanied
    Poet: Charles-Albert Congria
    Year: 1937
    Dedication: C. F. Ramuz
    Published: (1) V. Porchet & Cie., 1938, in *Hommages à
       C.–F. Ramuz;* (2) *Feuilles musicales et courrier suisse
       du disque* (Lausanne) March/April 1962, facsimile
       of holograph

P13 *Petites chansons*
    Medium: Songs with piano
    Poet: After popular Russian texts
    Year: 1913
    Alternate titles: (1) *Little songs;* (2) *Recollections of my
       childhood;* (3) *Souvenirs de mon enfance;* (4) *Piesenki;*
       (5) *Izy vospomianiǐ iunosheskikhy*
    Duration: 1'30"
    Notes: French translation by C. F. Ramuz; English
       translation by Robert Burness
    Contents: (1) Le petit pie (The magpie; Sorochenyka);
       (2) Le corbeau (The rook; Vorona); (3) Tchitcher-latcher
       (The jackdaw; Chichery iachery)
    Published: (1) Boosey & Hawkes, 1947, plate no. B&H
       16307; (2) Edition Russe de Musique, 192?, 1914,
       plate no. RMV 236, 342, 355

P14 *Petites chansons; voice & orchestra*
   Medium: Songs with orchestra
   Year: 1930
   Duration: 3'
   Published: (1) Edition Russe de Musique, 1934, plate no.
      RMV 518; (2) Boosey & Hawkes

Pétrouchka
   see *Petroushka* (P15)

P15 *Petroushka*
   Medium: Ballets; Orchestral music
   Year: 1911
   Alternate title: (1) *Pétrouchka*; (2) *Petrushka*
   Duration: 43'
   Dedication: Alexandre Benois
   First performance: Paris; Ballet Russe; Pierre Monteux,
      conductor; 13 June 1911
   Published: (1) Edition Russe de Musique, Breitkopf und
      Härtel, 1912, LC M61-2090; (2) W. W. Norton, 1967
      (Norton critical scores) ed. Charles E. Hamm, LC
      67-17012/M; (3) Edition Russe de Musique, Breitkopf
      und Härtel, 1912, plate no. RMV 348, miniature score,
      M61-2091; (4) Gosudarstvennyi Muzykal'noe izd-vo,
      1962, LC 63-52497/M; (5) Edwin F. Kalmus, 196?
      (Kalmus pocket scores, 79) LC 67-46811/M; (6) Boosey
      & Hawkes, 194? (Hawkes pocket scores, 574)
      LC 45-50536

P16 *Petroushka (1947)*
   Medium: Orchestral music; Ballets
   Year: 1946 [sic]
   Notes: Revised for reduced orchestra
   Published: (1) Boosey & Hawkes, 1948 (Hawkes pocket
      scores, 639); (2) Boosey & Hawkes, 1948, LC 48-21850

P17 *Petroushka (1947); piano, 4 hands*
  Medium: Piano music (4 hands)
  Notes: Arranged by the composer and Alexandre Benois
  Published: (1) Edition Russe de Musique, Boosey & Hawkes,
    1948, plate no. RMV 150, LC 49-15898

P18 *Petroushka; arr., orchestra*
  Medium: Orchestral music
  Notes: Arranged by Quinto Maganini
  Published: (1) Edition Musicus, 1941

P19 *Petroushka; arr., piano*
  Medium: Piano music
  Notes: Arranged by M. Mirkina and S. Pavchinskogo
  Published: (1) Muzyka, 1967, LC 67-51716/M

P20 *Petroushka. Chez Petroushka; arr., piano*
  Medium: Piano music
  Notes: Arranged by Frederick Block
  Published: (1) Marks Music Corporation, 1951
    (Kaleidoscope edition, 11507) LC 74-231236; (2) Marks
    Music Corporation, 1936 (Album of Igor Stravinsky
    masterpieces; Contemporary masterpieces, n. 9)

P21 *Petroushka. Danse de la ballerine; arr., women's voices,*
  violin & piano
  Medium: Choruses (Women's voices) with piano and violin
  Notes: Arranged by William Lester
  Published: (1) Breitkopf and Härtel, 1925, plate no.
  Dance of the ballerina 5 1/2

P22 *Petroushka. Danse des cochers et des palefreniers;*
  arr., women's voices & piano
  Medium: Choruses (Women's voices) with piano

62

Notes: Arranged by William Lester
Published: (1) Breitkopf and Härtel, 1925, plate no.
Dance of the coachmen 6 1/2

P23 *Petroushka. Danse russe; violin & piano*
Medium: Violin and piano music
Year: 1932
Notes: Arranged by the composer and Samuel Dushkin
Published: (1) Edition Russe de Musique, 1933, plate no.
RMV 565; (2) Edition Russe de Musique, Boosey &
Hawkes, 1933, plate no. B&H 16888; (3) Gosudarstvennyi
Muzykal'noe izd-vo, 1963

P24 *Petroushka. Danse russe; arr., piano*
Medium: Piano music
Notes: Arranged by Luis Sucra
Published: (1) Marks Music Corporation, 1936, 1935
(Album of Igor Stravinsky masterpieces; Contemporary
masterpieces, n. 9) plate no. 10619; (2) Marks Music
Corporation, 1935 (Edition A. Fassio) plate no. AF 10-04

P25 *Petroushka. Danse russe; arr., piano, 4 hands*
Medium: Piano music (4 hands)
Notes: Arranged by Felix Guenther
Published: (1) Marks Music Corporation, 1941
(Kaleidoscope edition, 11255)

P26 *Petroushka. Danse russe; arr., 2 pianos*
Medium: Piano music (2 pianos)
Notes: Arranged by Felix Guenther
Published: (1) Marks Music Corporation, 1941
(Kaleidoscope edition, 11266)

P27 *Petroushka. Danse russe; arr., 2 pianos, 8 hands*
Medium: Piano music (2 pianos, 8 hands)
Notes: Arranged by I. Bogomolov
Published: (1) Sovetskiĭ Kompozitor, 1962, published with
waltz from *War and peace* by Prokofiev

P28 *Petroushka. Fête populaire de la semaine grasse; arr., piano*
Medium: Piano music
Alternate title: *Danse de la foire*
Published: (1) Marks Music Corporation, 1941
(Kaleidoscope edition, 11508) LC 77-231269, arranged by
Frederick Block; (2) Marks Music Corporation, 1936,
1935 (Album of Igor Stravinsky masterpieces;
Contemporary masterpieces, n. 9) plate no. 10619,
arranged by Frederick Block; (3) Boosey & Hawkes,
1953, arranged by Victor Babin

P29 *Petroushka. Selections; piano*
Medium: Piano music
Year: 1921
Dedication: Artur Rubinstein
Contents: (1) Russian dance; (2) In Petroushka's cell;
(3) Shrove-tide fair
Published: (1) Edition Russe de Musique, 1922, plate no.
RMV 400; (2) Edition Russe de Musique, Boosey &
Hawkes, 1947, plate no. B&H 16301; (3) Gosudarstvennyi
Muzykal'noe izd-vo, 1963

P30 *Petroushka. Selections; arr., band*
Medium: Band music
Notes: Arranged by Maurice Gardner
Published: (1) Staff Music Publishing Co., 1955

P31 *Petroushka. Selections; arr., piano*
    Medium: Piano music
    Notes: Arranged by Théodore Szántó
    Published: (1) Edition Russe de Musique, 1922, plate no.
      RMV 399

P32 *Petroushka. Selections; arr., 2 pianos*
    Medium: Piano music (2 pianos)
    Notes: Arranged by Victor Babin
    Published: (1) Edition Russe de Musique, Boosey &
      Hawkes, 1953, LC M55-196

  Petrushka
  see *Petroushka* (P15)

P33 *Piano-rag music*
    Medium: Piano music
    Year: 1919
    Duration: 3'
    Dedication: Artur Rubinstein
    First performance: Lausanne; José Iturbi; 8 November 1919
    Published: (1) J. & W. Chester, 1920 (Chester library)
      plate no. JWC 2061

P34 *Pieces, clarinet*
    Medium: Clarinet music
    Year: 1919
    Duration: 3'45"
    Dedication: Warner Reinhart
    First performance: Lausanne; Edmond Allegra;
      8 November 1919
    Contents: Three movements, each identified by metronome
      markings, the first also called Sempre piano e molto
      tranquillo

Published: (1) Mercury Music Corporation, n.d. (Mercury wind instrument library) plate no. W-34; (2) J. & W. Chester, 1923, 1920, plate no. JWC 1551, LC 75-287428

P35 *Pièces, string quartet*
Medium: String quartets
Year: 1914
Alternate title: *P'esy i kontsertino*
Duration: 8'
Notes: Ed. F. H. Schneider; absorbed as the first three movements of *Etudes* for orchestra (E8)
Dedication: Ernest Ansermet
Contents: Three movements, with metronome indications
Published: (1) Muzyka, 1968, includes his *Concertino* (C28) LC 68-130660/M; (2) Muzyka, 1969, parts only, LC 70-227250; (3) Edition Russe de Musique, 1922, plate no. 402, LC M61-2087; (4) Boosey & Hawkes, 1922 (Hawkes pocket scores, 634) plate no. B&H 16313; (5) Boosey & Hawkes, 1947, plate no. B&H 184444, parts only

Pièces à la norvegiénne
see *Norwegian moods* (N3)

P36 *Pièces faciles, piano, 4 hands (1915)*
Medium: Piano music (4 hands)
Year: 1915
Duration: 3'
Notes: Absorbed by *Suite no. 2* (S31)
Dedication: Alfredo Casella, Erik Satie, Serge Diaghilev
First performance: Lausanne; José Iturbi, Igor Stravinsky, pianos; 8 November 1919
Contents: (1) March; (2) Waltz; (3) Polka
Published: (1) Ad. Henn, 1923, 1917, plate no. A67H; (2) J. & W. Chester, 1926, 1917, plate no. JWC 2910

P37 *Pièces faciles, piano, 4 hands (1915). No. 1: March; instrumental ensemble*
    Medium: Instrumental ensembles
    Year: 1915

P38 *Pièces faciles, piano, 4 hands (1915). No. 2: Waltz; instrumental septet*
    Medium: Septets

P39 *Pièces faciles, piano, 4 hands (1915). No. 3: Polka; cimbalom*
    Medium: Cimbalom music
    Year: 1915
    Dedication: Aladar Raiz
    Published: (1) *Feuilles musicales et courrier suisse du disque* (Lausanne) March/April 1962, facsimile of holograph

P41 *Pièces faciles, piano, 4 hands (1917)*
    Medium: Piano music (4 hands)
    Year: 1917
    Alternate title: *Easy pieces*
    Duration: 9'
    Notes: First four movements absorbed by his *Suite* no. 1 (S30), final movement absorbed by his *Suite* no. 2 (S31)
    Dedication: Eugenia Errazuriz
    First performance: Lausanne; José Iturbi, Igor Stravinsky, pianos; 8 November 1919
    Contents: (1) Andante; (2) Española; (3) Balalaika; (4) Napolitana; (5) Galop
    Published: (1) Ad. Henn, 1923, 1917, plate no. A72H; (2) J. & W. Chester, 1925, plate no. JWC 2909

P42 *Pièces faciles, piano, 4 hands (1915). No. 4: Napolitana; arr., piano*
    Medium: Piano music

Notes: Arranged by Gregory Stone
Published: (1) Marks Music Corporation, 1941
(Kaleidoscope edition, 11505)

P43 *Pièces faciles, piano, 4 hands (1915). No. 4: Napolitana;
arr., flute, oboe, 2 clarinets, bassoon, horn*
Medium: Wind sextets (Bassoon, clarinets, flute, horn, oboe)
Notes: Arranged by Gregory Stone
Published: (1) Abby Music Co., 1948, LC 48-21538

P44 *Pièces faciles, piano, 4 hands (1917). Selections;
chamber orchestra*
Medium: Chamber orchestra music
Alternate titles: (1) *Suite, chamber orchestra*; (2) *Dve suity*
Published: (1) Muzyka, 1967, LC 67-119258rev/M

Piesenki
see *Petites chansons* (P13)

Piesnia solovyia
see *Le chant du rossignol* (C13)

P45 *Poèmes de Verlaine, op. 9*
Medium: Songs (Medium voice) with piano
Poet: Paul Verlaine
Year: 1910
Notes: Russian translation by S. Mitusov; English and
German translations by M. D. Calvocoressi
Dedication: Gury Stravinsky
Contents: (1) Sagesse: Un grand sommeil noir; (2) La bonne
chanson: La lune blanche
Published: (1) Jurgenson, 1911, plate no. 34547-34548;
(2) Boosey & Hawkes

P46 *Poèmes de Verlaine, op. 9 (1953)*
Medium: Songs (Medium voice) with piano

Year: 1953
Published: (1) Boosey & Hawkes, 1955, 1954, plate no.
B&H 17408, 17409

P47 *Poèmes de Verlaine, op. 9; voice & orchestra*
Medium: Songs with orchestra
Year: 1951
Published: (1) Boosey & Hawkes, 1953, plate no. 17408,
17409; LC M54-1765

P48 *Poems of Balmont*
Medium: Songs (High voice) with piano
Poet: K. Balmont
Year: 1911
Duration: 2'30"
Notes: French translation by M. D. Calvocoressi; English
translation by Robert Craft; German translation by
Berthold Feiwel
Dedication: Ludmilla Beliankin and the composer's mother
Contents: (1) The flower (Nezobudochka-tsvietocheky);
(2) The dove (Goluby)
Published: (1) Edition Russe de Musique, 1912,
plate no. RMV 130

P49 *Poems of Balmont (revised)*
Medium: Songs (High voice) with piano
Year: 1947
Published: (1) Edition Russe de Musique, Boosey &
Hawkes, 1947, plate no. B&H 16305; (2) Boosey &
Hawkes, 1956, plate no. 18105, LC M57-1476

P50 *Poems of Balmont; voice & chamber orchestra*
Medium: Songs (High voice) with chamber orchestra
Year: 1954

Published: (1) Boosey & Hawkes, 1955, plate no.
B&H 17701, LC M57-861

P51 *Poésie de la lyrique japonaise*
Medium: Songs (High voice) with piano
Poet: A. Brandta
Year: 1913
Alternate title: *Japanese lyrics*
Duration: 3'30"
Notes: French translation by Maurice Delage; English
translation by Robert Burness; German translation by
Ernst Roth
Dedication: Maurice Delage, Florent Schmitt, Maurice Ravel
First performance: Paris; Société Musicale Indépendante;
11 January 1914
Contents: (1) Akahito (Descendons au jardin);
(2) Mazatsumi (Avril paraît); (3) Tsaraiuki (Qu'aperçoit-
on si blanc au loin?)
Published: (1) Edition Russe de Musique, 1913, plate no.
R.M.V. 200-201, LC M61-2154rev; (2) Boosey & Hawkes,
plate no. B&H 18105

P52 *Poésie de la lyrique japonaise; voice & chamber orchestra*
Medium: Songs (High voice) with chamber orchestra
Published: (1) Edition Russe de Musique, 1913; (2) Boosey
& Hawkes, 1955, plate no. B&H 17701, LC M57-861

Polka
see *Pièces faciles, piano, 4 hands (1915). No. 3:
Polka; cimbalom* (P39)

Potselvi fei
see *Le baiser de la fée. Deuxième tableau. Selection;
violin & piano* (B11)

P53 *Praeludium, jazz ensemble*
    Medium: Jazz ensembles
    Year: 1937
    Duration: 2′
    Published: (1) Boosey & Hawkes, 1968, plate no. B&H
      19718, LC 77-203148

P54 *Praeludium, jazz ensemble (1953)*
    Medium: Jazz ensembles
    Year: 1953
    Notes: Orchestration includes string parts
    First performance: Los Angeles; Evenings on the
      Roof Concerts; Robert Craft, conductor;
      18 October 1953

P55 *Praeludium, jazz ensemble; piano*
    Medium: Piano music

P56 *Pribaoutki*
    Medium: Songs (Medium voice) with chamber orchestra
    Poet: After popular Russian texts
    Year: 1914
    Alternate title: (1) *Chansons plaisantes*; (2) *Scherzlieder*
    Duration: 5′
    Notes: French translation by C. F. Ramuz, German
      translation by R. St. Hoffmann
    Dedication: To the composer's wife
    First performance: Paris; Salle Gaveau; May 1919
    Contents: (1) L'oncle Armand (Onkel Peter; Kornillo;
      Kornilo); (2) Le four (Marianna; Natasha; Natashka);
      (3) Le colonel (Der Oberst; The colonel; Polkovniky);
      (4) Le vieux et le lièvre (Der Greis und der Hase;
      The old man and the hare; Storechy i zaiatsy)

Published: (1) J. & W. Chester, 1917, LC 44-49809rev/M;
(2) Ad. Henn, 1917, LC 62-37363/M; (3) Wiener
Philharmonischer Verlag, 1926, 1917 (Philharmonia
Partituren, 293) plate no. W.Ph.V. 293 JWC 15a

P57 *Pribaoutki; voice & piano*
Medium: Songs with piano
Published: (1) J. & W. Chester, 1924 (Edition Chester, 125)
plate no. J.W.C. 3825, LC M61-2123; (2) B. Schott's
Söhne, plate no. 2053; (3) Ad. Henn, 1923, plate no. A70H

P58 *Pulcinella*
Medium: Ballets; Orchestral music
Year: 1920
Duration: 35'
Notes: Based on music by Giovanni Battista Pergolesi
First performance: Paris; Ballet Russe; Ernest Ansermet,
conductor; 15 May 1920
Contents: Eighteen movements
Published: (1) Edition Russe de Musique, 1924, plate no.
RMV 410; (2) Boosey & Hawkes

P59 *Pulcinella (1965)*
Medium: Ballets; Orchestral music
Year: 1965
Published: (1) Boosey & Hawkes, 1966, LC 67-44885/M

P60 *Pulcinella; piano*
Medium: Piano music
Published: (1) J. & W. Chester, 1920, plate no. JWC 9707,
LC M61-2194

P61 *Pulcinella (Suite)*
Medium: Orchestral music
Year: 1920

Duration: 22′
Notes: Ed. by Albert Spaulding
First performance: Boston; Boston Symphony Orchestra;
Pierre Monteux, conductor; 22 December 1922
Contents: Eleven movements
Published: (1) Edition Russe de Musique, 1924, plate no.
RMV 409; (2) Edition Russe de Musique,
Boosey & Hawkes

Pulcinella (Suite); violin & piano
see *Suite, violin & piano* (S32)
Suite italienne; violin & piano (S33)

Pulcinella (Suite); violoncello & piano
see *Suite italienne; violoncello & piano* (S34)

P62 *Pulcinella (Suite, 1947)*
Medium: Orchestral music
Year: 1947
Published: (1) Boosey & Hawkes, 1947 (Hawkes pocket
scores, 632) plate no. B&H 16332

P63 *Pulcinella (Suite, 1949)*
Medium: Orchestral music
Year: 1949
Published: (1) Edition Russe de Musique, Boosey &
Hawkes, 1949, LC 49-25581

P63.5 *Pulcinella. Con queste paroline; voice & piano*
Medium: Songs (Low voice) with piano
Published: (1) J. & W. Chester, 1925, plate no. JWC 3946

P64 *Pulcinella. Gavotta con variazioni; piano*
Medium: Piano music
Published: (1) J. & W. Chester, 1920, LC M61-2197

P65 *Pulcinella. Scherzino; piano*
Medium: Piano music
Published: (1) J. & W. Chester, 1920, LC M61-2196

P66 *Pulcinella. Selections; violin & piano*
Medium: Violin and piano music
Published: (1) Boosey & Hawkes

R1 *Ragtime*
Medium: Instrumental ensembles
Year: 1918
Duration: 4'30"
Notes: LC cites piano reduction as original version, in
distinction from the title page designation
Dedication: Eugenia Errazuriz
First performance: London; Philharmonic Quartet, and
others; Arthur Bliss, conductor; 27 April 1920
Published: (1) Editions de la Sirène, 1919; (2) B. Schott's
Söhne, plate no. 3568; (3) J. & W. Chester, 1920,
plate no. W.Ph.V. 291 JWC 22a, LC M61-2319;
(4) J. & W. Chester, 1923, plate no. JWC 22; (5) Wiener
Philharmonischer Verlag, 1924, 1920 (Philharmonia
Partituren, 291) plate no. W.Ph.V. 291 JWC 22a,
LC M61-2319

R2 *Ragtime; piano*
Medium: Piano music
Date: 1919
Published: (1) J. & W. Chester, 1922, 1919, plate no.
JWC 2071; (2) Editions de la Sirène, 1919,
plate no. ED4LS

R3 *The rake's progress*
Medium: Operas

Poet: Wystan Hugh Auden and Chester Kallman
Year: 1951
Alternate title: (1) *Der Wüstling;* (2) *Le libertin;*
(3) *La carriera d'un libertino*
Duration: 150'
Notes: German translation by Fritz Schroeder; French
translation by André de Badet; Italian translation by
Rinaldo Küfferle
First performance: Venice; Teatro la Fenice; orchestra
and chorus of Teatro alla Scala; Igor Stravinsky,
conductor; 11 September 1951
Published: (1) Boosey & Hawkes, 1951 (Hawkes pocket
scores, 739) plate no. 17853; (2) Boosey & Hawkes, 1951,
full score, LC 52-42777

R4 *The rake's progress. Libretto*
Medium: Librettos
Published: (1) Boosey & Hawkes, 1951, in English,
LC 52-27398; (2) Boosey & Hawkes, 1951, in German,
LC 52-43528

R5 *The rake's progress. Piano-vocal score*
Medium: Piano-vocal scores
Published: (1) Boosey & Hawkes, 1951, plate no. B&H
17088, text in English and German, LC 52-42315

R6 *The rake's progress. Lullaby; 2 recorders*
Medium: Recorder music (2 recorders)
Published: (1) Boosey & Hawkes, 1960

Raoul Dufy in memoriam
see *Double canon, string quartet* (D4)

Recollections of my childhood
see *Petites chansons* (P13)

R7 *Renard*
   Medium: Operas
   Poet: Igor Stravinsky, after popular Russian texts
   Year: 1916
   Alternate title: (1) *Reynard*; (2) *Baïka*
   Duration: 20'
   Notes: French translation by C. F. Ramuz; German
      translation by Rupert Koller; English translation
      by Rollo M. Meyers
   Dedication: Princess Edmond de Polignac
   First performance: Paris; Ballet Russe; 18 May 1922
   Published: (1) Ad. Henn, 1917; (2) J. & W. Chester,
      1930, 1917, plate no. W.Ph.V. 176 J.W.C. 60a, LC
      44-27504rev; (3) Wiener Philharmonischer Verlag, 1928
      (Philharmonia Partituren, 176) plate no. W.Ph.V. 176,
      LC M61-1716; (4) Boosey & Hawkes, plate no. B&H
      1011; (5) B. Schott's Söhne, n.d.?, plate no. BSS 3493,
      disclaimed by publisher

R8 *Renard. Piano-vocal score*
   Medium: Piano-vocal scores
   Published: (1) B. Schott's Söhne, text in French and German;
      (2) Ad. Henn, 1923, plate no. A66H; (3) J. & W.
      Chester, 1926

R9 *Requiem canticles*
   Medium: Choruses with orchestra
   Year: 1966
   Published: (1) Boosey & Hawkes, 1967, LC 67-55032/M;
      (2) Boosey & Hawkes, 1967 (Hawkes pocket scores, 738)

R10 *Requiem canticles. Piano-vocal score*
   Medium: Piano-vocal scores
   Published: (1) Boosey & Hawkes, 1967, LC 67-55031/M

Reynard
  see *Renard* (R7)

The rite of spring
  see *Le sacre du printemps* (S1)

R11 *Le roi des étoiles*
  Medium: Choruses (Men's voices) with orchestra
  Poet: K. Balmont
  Year: 1912
  Alternate title: (1) *Zvezdoliki*; (2) *Zviezdolokiĭ*
  Duration: 6′
  Notes: French translation by M. D. Calvocoressi
  Dedication: Claude Debussy
  First performance: Bruxelles; Institut Nationale de
    Radiodiffusion Belge; Franz André, conductor;
    19 April 1939
  Published: (1) Jurgenson, 1913; (2) Robert Forberg,
    1913, 1911, plate no. 36729

R12 *Le roi des étoiles. Piano-vocal score*
  Medium: Piano-vocal scores
  Published: (1) Robert Forberg, 1911, plate no. 36731;
    (2) J. & W. Chester, 19??, plate no. JWC 36732,
    disclaimed by publisher

La ronde des princesses
  see entries for *L'oiseau de feu* (O51-O55)

Ronde printanière
  see *Le sacre du printemps. Ronde printanière; arr.,*
    piano (S8)

R13 *Le rossignol*
  Medium: Operas
  Poet: S. Mitusov, after Hans Christian Andersen

Year: 1914

Alternate title: (1) *The nightingale*; (2) *Die Nachtigall*; (3) *Solovei*

Duration: 45'

Notes: English translations by Basil T. Timothieff and Charles C. Hayne, and by Robert Craft; German translations by Liesbeth Weinhold, and by A. Elukhen and Berthold Feiwel; Music later used also for *Le chant du rossignol* (C13)

Dedication: S. Mitusov

First performance: Paris; Ballet Russe, Pierre Monteux, conductor; 26 May 1914

Published: (1) Edition Russe de Musique, 1923, plate no. RMV 241; (2) Boosey & Hawkes (Hawkes pocket scores, 738)

R14 *Le rossignol (1962)*

Medium: Operas

Year: 1962

Notes: French translation by M. D. Calvocoressi; English translation by Robert Craft; new German translations by A. Elukhen and Berthold Feiwel

Published: (1) Boosey & Hawkes, 1962, text in English, French, German and Russian, LC 62-45725/M; (2) Boosey & Hawkes, 1962, miniature score, LC 62-45728/M

R15 *Le rossignol. Piano-vocal score*

Medium: Piano-vocal scores

Published: (1) Edition Russe de Musique, Boosey & Hawkes, plate no. B&H 17187; (2) Boosey & Hawkes, 1961, LC M61-2499

R16 *Le rossignol. Chant du rossignol; arr., piano*
  Medium: Piano music
  Notes: Arranged by Frederick Block
  Published: (1) Marks Music Corporation, 1941
    (Kaleidoscope edition, 11518) LC 79-231256; (2) Marks
    Music Corporation, 1936 (Album of Igor Stravinsky
    masterpieces; Contemporary masterpieces, n. 9)

R17 *Le rossignol. Marche chinoise; arr., piano*
  Medium: Piano music
  Notes: Arranged by Théodore Szántó
  Published: (1) Edition Russe de Musique, 1922,
    plate no. RMV 346

R18 *Le rossignol. Selections. Piano-vocal score*
  Medium: Piano-vocal scores
  Published: (1) Edition Russe de Musique, 1924,
    plate no. 241 241a

  Russian maiden's song
    see *Mavra. Drug moǐ milyǐ; violin & piano* (M5);
    Mavra. Drug moǐ milyǐ; voice & piano (M8)

R19 *Russian peasant songs; women's voices, unaccompanied*
  Medium: Choruses (Women's voices), Unaccompanied
  Poet: After Afanasiev's collection of popular Russian texts
  Year: 1917
  Alternate title: (1) *Saucers*; (2) *Unterschale*; (3) *Podliudnyiia*
  Duration: 3'
  Notes: German text by Hermann Roth
  First performance: Genève; Vassily Kibalchich,
    conductor; 1917

Contents: (1) On saints' day in Chigaskh (Près de l'église
à Chigisak; Beim Heiland von Tschigissi; U spasa vy
Chigisakhy); (2) Ovsen (Herbst; Ovzeny); (3) The pike
(Le brochet; Der Hecht; Shchuka); (4) Master Portly
(Monsieur Ventru; Freund Dicksack; Puzishchi)
Published: (1) B. Schott's Söhne, 1930, plate no. C32640;
(2) J. & W. Chester, 1938, 1932; (3) Marks Music
Corporation, 1950 (Arthur Jordan choral series, 27)
plate no. 12734, piano reduction and ed. Felix Greissle
for four-part men's or women's chorus

R20 *Russian peasant songs; women's voices & 4 horns*
Medium: Choruses (Women's voices) with 4 horns
Year: 1954
Duration: 3'40"
First Performance: Los Angeles; Monday Evening Concerts;
Robert Craft, conductor; 11 October, 1954
Published: (1) J. & W. Chester, 1958, LC M58-1876;
(2) B. Schott's Söhne, 1957, plate no. C 39491, score;
(3) B. Schott's Söhne, 1957, plate no. C 39491c,
horn parts

Russian songs
see *Songs (1954)* (S25)
Chants Russes (C18)

Sacrae cantiones
see Z8

S1 *Le sacre du printemps*
Medium: Ballets; Orchestral music
Year: 1913
Alternate titles: (1) *The rite of spring*; (2) *Vesna
sviashchennaia*
Duration: 34'

Dedication: Nicolas Roerich

First performance: Paris; Ballet Russe; Pierre Monteux, conductor; 29 May 1913

Published: (1) Edition Russe de Musique, 1921, plate no. RMV 197b, LC M61-2084; (2) Boosey and Hawkes, 1921 (Hawkes pocket scores, 638) plate no. B&H 16333; (3) Boosey and Hawkes, 1921?, full score; (4) Edwin F. Kalmus, 1933 (Kalmus miniature scores, 78), LC 44-49107; (5) Boosey and Hawkes, 1969, facsimile with commentary by Robert Craft, LC 79-6004; (6) Muzyka, 1965, LC 66-56024/M

S2 *Le sacre du printemps; piano*
Medium: Piano music

S3 *Le sacre du printemps; piano, 4 hands*
Medium: Piano music (4 hands)
Published: (1) Edition Russe de Musique, 1913, plate no. RMV 196; (2) Muzyka, 1972

S4 *Le sacre du printemps. Les augures printaniers; arr., piano*
Medium: Piano music
Notes: Arranged by Frederick Block
Published: (1) E. B. Marks Music Corporation, 1941 (Kaleidoscope edition, 11510) LC 73-231312

S5 *Le sacre du printemps. Danse des adolescents; arr., piano*
Medium: Piano music
Notes: Arranged by Frederick Block
Published: (1) Marks Music Corporation, 1941 (Kaleidoscope edition, 11510-5) LC 73-231312; (2) Marks Music Corporation, 1936 (Album of Igor Stravinsky masterpieces; Contemporary master-pieces, n. 9)

S6 *Le sacre du printemps. Danse sacrale (1943)*
  Medium: Orchestral music
  Year: 1943
  Duration: 9′
  Published: (1) Associated Music Publishers, 1945,
    LC 46-19830

S7 *Le sacre du printemps. Jeux des cités rivales; arr., piano*
  Medium: Piano music
  Alternate title: *Tourneys of rival tribes*
  Notes: Arranged by Frederick Block
  Published: (1) E. B. Marks Music Corporation, 1941
    (Kaleidoscope edition, 11506) LC 73-231268

S8 *Le sacre du printemps. Ronde printanière; arr., piano*
  Medium: Piano music
  Notes: Arranged by Frederick Block
  Published: (1) E. B. Marks Music Corporation, 1941
    (Kaleidoscope edition, 11509-2) LC 77-231313

  Sacred choruses
    see *Credo (1964)* (C45)

  Saucers
    see *Russian peasant songs; women's voices,
      unaccompanied* (R19)

S9 *Scènes de ballet*
  Medium: Ballets; Orchestral music
  Year: 1944
  Duration: 18′
  Commission: Billy Rose
  First performance: Philadelphia; Maurice Abravanel,
    conductor; 1945

Contents: (1) Introduction; andante; (2) Danses;
moderato; (3) Variations, con moto; (4) Pantomime;
lento; (5) Pas de deux; adagio; (6) Pantomime;
agitato ma tempo giusto; (7) Variation; risoluto; (8)
Variation; andantino; (9) Danses; con moto; (10)
Apothèse; poco meno mosso
Published: (1) Associated Music Publishers, 1951, 1945,
plate no. AC 194440, LC 46-1341

S10 *Scènes de ballet; arr., piano*
Medium: Piano music
Notes: Reduction by Ingolf Dahl

Scherzino
see *Pulcinella. Scherzino; arr., piano* (P65)

Scherzlieder
see *Pribaoutki* (P56)

Scherzo, violin & piano
see *L'oiseau de feu. Scherzo; violin & piano* (O33)

S11 *Scherzo à la russe, jazz ensemble*
Medium: Jazz ensembles
Year: 1944
Duration: 4′
Dedication: Paul Whiteman
First performance: Blue Network broadcast; Paul
Whiteman, conductor, 1944
Published: (1) Chappell, 1949

S12 *Scherzo à la russe, jazz ensemble; orchestra*
Medium: Orchestral music
Year: 1944
Duration: 4′

First performance: San Francisco; San Francisco Symphony
Orchestra; Igor Stravinsky, conductor; March 1946
Published: (1) Chappell, 1945; (3) Associated Music
Publishers, 1945, plate no. AC 194552, LC 47-25538;
(3) B. Schott's Söhne, 1954 (Edition Schott, 4553)
plate no. BSS 38949a

S13 *Scherzo à la russe, jazz ensemble; piano*
Medium: Piano music
Published: (1) Associated Music Publishers, 1945, plate
no. AC-19455

S14 *Scherzo à la russe, jazz ensemble; 2 pianos*
Medium: Piano music (2 pianos)
Published: (1) Schott (London), 1945 (Edition Schott,
10646) plate no. 6184; (2) Associated Music Publishers,
1945, plate no. AC 19455, LC 47-28183

S15 *Scherzo fantastique, orchestra, op. 3*
Medium: Orchestral music
Year: 1908
Duration: 16'
Notes: In 1930 the composer reduced the three harp parts
for two players.
Dedication: Alexander Siloti
First performance: St. Petersburg; Alexandre Siloti,
conductor; 6 February 1909
Published: (1) Jurgenson, 1909?, plate no. 32930,
LC M61-2093; (2) B. Schott's Söhne, 1931 (Edition
Schott, 3501) plate no. BSS 32953, also issued in series
Musik des 20. Jahrhunderts, LC M61-2074; (3)
Associated Music Publishers, 1931 (Edition Schott, 3501)

S16 *Scherzo fantastique, orchestra, op. 3; arr., piano*
Medium: Piano music
Notes: Arranged by Gabriel Grovlez
Published: (1) Jurgenson, 191?

S17 *Septet, piano, winds & strings*
Medium: Septets
Year: 1953
Dedication: Dumbarton Oaks Research Library and
  Collection
First performance: Washington; Igor Stravinsky,
  conductor; 23 January 1953
Contents: (1) metronomic tempo indication; (2)
  Passacaglia; (3) Gigue
Published: (1) Boosey & Hawkes, 1953 (Hawkes pocket
  scores, 682) plate no. B&H 17447, LC M54-2341

S18 *Septet, piano, winds & strings; 2 pianos*
Medium: Piano music (2 pianos)
Published: (1) Boosey & Hawkes, 1953

S19 *Serenade, piano, A*
Medium: Piano music
Year: 1925
Duration: 12'
Notes: Ed. by Albert Spaulding
Dedication: To the composer's wife
Contents: (1) Hymne; (2) Romanza; (3) Rondoletto; (4)
  Cadenza finale
Published: (1) Edition Russe de Musique, 1926; (2) Boosey
  & Hawkes, 1947, plate no. 16303

S20 *A Sermon, a narrative and a prayer*
Medium: Cantatas
Year: 1961

Duration: 16'

Dedication: Paul Sacher

First performance: Basel; Basler Kammerorchester; Paul
  Sacher, conductor; 23 February 1962

Published: (1) Boosey & Hawkes, 1961 (Hawkes pocket
  scores, 733) plate no. B&H 18784, LC M61-2226; (2)
  Boosey & Hawkes, 1961, full score

S21 *A sermon, a narrative and a prayer. Piano-vocal score*
  Medium: Piano-vocal scores
  Published: (1) Boosey & Hawkes, 1961, plate no. B&H
    18874, LC M 61-2500

Simvol, viery
  see *Credo* (C43)

The sleeping beauty
  see Z3-Z4

Sochineniia dlia fortepiano
  see *Works, instrumental. Selections. Sochineniia dlia
    fortepiano* (W2)

The soldier's tale
  see *L'histoire du soldat* (H1)

Solovei
  see *Le rossignol* (R13)

S22 *Sonata, piano (1904), F-sharp minor*
  Medium: Piano music
  Year: 1904
  Dedication: Nicolas Richter
  First performance: St. Petersburg; Nicholas Richter, piano;
    9 February 1905
  Contents: (1) Allegro; (2) Andante; (3) Scherzo; (4) Finale

S23 *Sonata, piano (1924)*
   Medium: Piano music
   Year: 1924
   Duration: 10′
   Notes: Ed. by Albert Spaulding
   Dedication: Princess Edmond de Polignac
   First performance: Donnaueschingen; July 1925
   Contents: (1) metronomic tempo indication; (2) Adagietto;
      (3) metronomic tempo indication
   Published: (1) Edition Russe de Musique, 1925, plate no.
      RMV 417; (2) Boosey & Hawkes, 1925, plate no.
      B&H 16498

S24 *Sonata, 2 pianos*
   Medium: Piano music (2 pianos)
   Year: 1944
   Duration: 11′
   Notes: Also published in *Sochineniia dlia fortepiano* (*see*
      W2)
   First performance: Madison, Wisconsin; Nadia Boulanger,
      Richard Johnson, pianos; July 1944
   Contents: (1) Moderato; (2) Theme with variations; (3)
      Allegretto
   Published: (1) Chappell, 1945; (2) Associated Music
      Publishers, 1945, plate no. AC 194423, LC 45-17691;
      (3) B. Schott's Söhne, 1953 (Edition Schott, 4015) plate
      no. BSS 38482

Song of the flea
   see Z2

The song of the nightingale
   see *Le chant du rossignol* (C13)

Song of the Volga boatmen
   see Z5

S25 *Songs (1954)*
Medium: Songs (high voice) with flute, harp and guitar
Year: 1954
Alternate title: *Russian songs*
Duration: 4'30"
Notes: Nos. 1 and 2 are from *Chants russes,* nos. 3 and 4
(*see* C18); nos. 3 and 4 are from *Histoires pour enfants,*
nos. 3 and 2 (*see* H8); English translation by Robert
Craft and Rosa Newmarch
First performance: Los Angeles; Monday Evening Concerts;
Robert Craft, conductor; 21 February 1955
Contents: (1) The drake; (2) A Russian spiritual; (3)
Geese and swans; (4) Tilimbom
Published: (1) J. & W. Chester, 1955, plate no. J.C.W. 3831,
LC M57-1185rev (as *Chants russes. Selections; arr.*)

S26 *Songs from William Shakespeare*
Medium: Songs (High voice) with flute, clarinet and viola
Poet: William Shakespeare
Year: 1953
Duration: 6'30"
First performance: Los Angeles; Robert Craft, narrator;
8 March 1954
Contents: (1) Musick to heare; (2) Full fadom five; (3) When
daisies pied
Published: (1) Boosey & Hawkes, 1954 (Hawkes pocket
scores, 689) plate no. B&H 17493, LC M54-2100;
(2) Boosey & Hawkes, full score

S27 *Songs from William Shakespeare; voice & piano*
Medium: Songs (Medium voice) with piano
Poet: William Shakespeare
Published: (1) Boosey & Hawkes, 1954, LC M54-2101

Souvenirs de mon enfance
    see *Petites chansons* (P13)

S28 *Souvenir d'une marche boche*
    Medium: Piano music
    Year: 1915
    Published: (1) Macmillan & Co., 1916; facsimile in *The book of the homeless; le livre des sans-foyer,* ed. Edith Wharton*

Spanisches Liederbuch
    see Z18

The star-spangled banner
    see Z15-Z17

A Stravinsky suite
    see *Works, piano, 4 hands. Selections: arr., band. A Stravinsky Suite* (W4)

Studies, orchestra
    see *Etudes, orchestra* (E8)

Studies, piano
    see *Etudes, piano, op. 7* (E12)

Study, piano
    see *Etude, piano* (E7)

Suite, chamber orchestra
    see *Pièces faciles, piano, 4 hands (1917). Selections; chamber orchestra* (P44)

S29 *Suites, orchestra, nos. 1 & 2*
    Medium: Orchestral music
    Alternate title: Dve suity
    Published: (1) Muzyka, 1967 LC 67-119258rev/M

S30 *Suite, orchestra, no. 1*
Medium: Orchestral music
Year: 1925
Duration: 5'
Notes: Suite is orchestration of *Pièces faciles* (*see* P41)
Contents: (1) Andante; (2) Napolitana; (3) Española;
(4) Balalaika
Published: (1) J. & W. Chester, 1926, plate no. JWC 56b;
(2) Wiener Philharmonischer Verlag, 1927 (Philharmonia
Partituren, 172) plate no. W.Ph.V. 172, LC M61-1596rev

S31 *Suite, orchestra, no. 2*
Medium: Orchestral music
Year: 1921
Duration: 7'
Notes: Suite is orchestration of *Pièces faciles* (*see* P36 and
P41)
Contents: (1) March; (2) Waltz; (3) Polka; (4) Galop
Published: (1) J. & W. Chester, 1925, plate no. JWC 51;
(2) B. Schott's Söhne, n.d.?, plate no. BSS 3470,
disclaimed by the publisher; (3) Wiener Philharmonischer
Verlag, 1925 (Philharmonia Partituren, 295), plate no.
W.Ph.V. 295, LC 68-42456/M (as *Pièces faciles, piano
(4 hands); arr.*); (4) J. & W. Chester, 1925, plate no.
J.W.C. 51, full score; (5) J. & W. Chester, 1925,
miniature score, LC 68-42503/m

S32 *Suite, violin & piano*
Medium: violin and piano music
Year: 1925
Subtitle: D'après des thèmes, fragments et morceaux de
Giambattista Pergolesi
Notes: Based on nos. 1, 2, 12, 15, 17, and 18 of *Pulcinella*
(*see* P58)

Dedication: Paul Kochanski

Contents: (1) Introduzione; (2) Serenata; (3) Tarantella; (4) Gavotta con due variazioni; (5) Minuetto e finale

Published: (1) Edition Russe de Musique, 1926, LC 68-41762/M; (2) Bossey & Hawkes, n.d.?

S33 *Suite italienne, violin & piano*

Medium: Violin and piano music

Year: 1933 ca.

Alternate title: *Pulcinella suite, violin & piano*

Notes: Arranged by the composer and Samuel Dushkin on movements from *Pulcinella* (*see* P38)

Contents: (1) Introduzione; (2) Serenata; (3) Tarantella; (4) Gavotta con due variazioni; (5) Scherzino; (6) Menuetto e finale

Published: (1) Edition Russe de Musique, 1934, plate no. R.M.V. 428; (2) Boosey & Hawkes, 1947, 1934, plate no. B&H 17009

S34 *Suite italienne, violoncello & piano*

Medium: Violoncello and piano music

Year: 1932

Alternate title: *Pulcinella suite, violoncello & piano*

Notes: Arranged by the composer and Gregor Piatigorsky on movements from *Pulcinella* (see P58)

Contents: (1) Introduzione; (2) Serenata; (3) Aria; (4) Tarantella; (5) Minuetto e finale

Published: (1) Edition Russe de Musique, 1934, LC 68-41671/M; (2) Boosey & Hawkes, 1934, plate no. B&H 16350; (3) Muzyka, 1968

Summer moon

see *L'oiseau de feu. La ronde des princesses; arr., voice & piano* (O31)

Supplications
see *L'oiseau de feu: Supplications; arr., piano* (O38-O39)

Svadebka
see *Les noces* (N1)

S35 *Symphonie de psaumes*
Medium: Symphonies; Cantatas
Poet: Biblical text
Year: 1930
Altenate title: *Symphony of Psalms*
Duration: 23'
Commission: Serge Koussevitsky
Dedication: Boston Symphony Orchestra
First performance: Bruxelles; Palais des Beaux Arts; Société
    Philharmonique de Bruxelles; Ernest Ansermet,
    conductor; 13 December 1930
Contents: Metronomic tempo indications for three
    movements
Published: (1) Edition Russe de Musique, 1931, plate
    no. RMV 517; (2) Boosey & Hawkes, n.d.? (3) Muzyka,
    1969, LC 77-229613

S36 *Symphonie de psaumes. Piano-vocal score*
Medium: Piano-vocal scores; Cantatas
Year: 1930 ca.
Notes: Reduction by Sviatoslav Stravinsky
Published: (1) Edition Russe de Musique, 1930

S37 *Symphonie de psaumes (1948)*
Medium: Symphonies; Cantatas
Year: 1948
Published: (1) Boosey & Hawkes, 1948 (Hawkes pocket
    scores, 637) plate no. 16328, LC 48-23067rev; (2) Boosey
    & Hawkes, 1948, full score, LC 48-23066rev

S38 *Symphonie de psaumes (1948). Piano-vocal score*
Medium: Piano-vocal scores
Notes: Reduction by Soulima Stravinsky
Published: (1) Edition Russe de Musique, Boosey & Hawkes, 1948, LC 49-12167; (2) International Music Co., 196?, plate no. 1618, LC M60-2489

S39 *Symphonies d'instruments à vent* ⬧
Medium: Band music
Year: 1920
Alternate title: *Tombeau de Claude Debussy*
Duration: 12'
Dedication: In memoriam Claude Debussy
First performance: London; Serge Koussevitsky; 10 June 1921

S40 *Symphonies d'instruments à vent (1947)*
Medium: Band music
Year: 1947
Published: (1) Boosey & Hawkes, 1952 (Hawkes pocket scores, 672) plate no. B&H 17144, LC M54-1909; (2) Boosey & Hawkes, 1952, full score

S41 *Symphonies d'instruments à vent; arr., piano*
Medium: Piano music
Notes: Reduction by Arthur Lourié
Published: (1) Edition Russe de Musique, 1926

S42 *Symphonies d'instruments à vent. Finale, piano*
Medium: Piano music
Published: (1) La revue musicale, 1920

S43 *Symphony, C*
Medium: Symphonies
Year: 1940

Duration: 30'

Dedication: Chicago Symphony Orchestra

First performance: Chicago, Chicago Symphony Orchestra; Igor Stravinsky, conductor; 7 November 1940

Contents: (1) Moderato alla breve; (2) Larghetto concertante; (3) Allegretto; (4) Largo; tempo giusto, alla breve

Published: (1) B. Schott's Söhne, 1973, 1948 (Edition Schott, 3536) plate no. BSS 36032a, miniature score, also issued in series Musik des 20. Jahrhunderts; (2) Associated Music Publishers, 1948 (Edition Schott, 3501) LC 49-51806; (3) B. Schott's Söhne, 1949 (Edition Schott, 3840) plate no. BSS 36032, full score

S44 *Symphony, E-flat major, op. 1*

Medium: Symphonies

Year: 1907

Duration: 30'

Dedication: Nikolai Rimsky-Korsakov

First performance: St. Petersburg; Russian Symphony Orchestra; Felix Blumenfeld, conductor; 22 January 1908

Contents: (1) Allegro moderato; (2) Scherzo, allegretto; (3) Largo; (4) Finale, allegro moderato

S45 *Symphony, E-flat major, op. 1 (1914)*

Medium: Symphonies

Year: 1914

First performance: Montreux; Ernest Ansermet, conductor; 2 April 1914

Published: (1) Jurgenson, 1914, plate no. 36664; (3) Edwin F. Kalmus, n.d.; (3) Robert Forberg, 1914, plate no. 6828; (4) C. F. Peters, n.d., plate no. 36664; (6) Boosey & Hawkes, n.d.?

S46 *Symphony, E-flat major, op. 1; arr., piano, 4 hands*
  Medium: Piano music (4 hands)
  Notes: Arranged by A. Gilajew
  Published: (1) Robert Forberg, n.d.?; (2) Gosudarstvennyi
    Muzykal'noe izd-vo, 1928

S47 *Symphony (1945)*
  Medium: Symphonies
  Year: 1945
  Alternate title: *Symphony in three movements*
  Duration: 24'
  Dedication: New York Philharmonic-Symphony Society
  First performance: New York Philharmonic; Igor
    Stravinsky, conductor; 24 January 1946
  Contents: (1) metronomic tempo indication; (2) Andante;
    (3) Con moto
  Published: (1) Associated Music Publishers, 1946 (Edition
    Schott, 99) full score, LC 47-4165rev; (2) B. Schott's
    Söhne, 1951 (Edition Schott, 4075) plate no. BSS
    37675a, also issued in series Musik des 20. Jahrhunderts;
    (3) E. Eulenberg, 1946 (Edition Eulenberg, ETP 574)
    plate no. BSS 37675, LC 67-46817/M; (4) Associated
    Music Publishers, 1946 (Edition Schott, 4075)
    miniature score; (5) B. Schott's Söhne, 1951 (Edition
    Schott, 99) plate no. BSS 37675, full score

Symphony of Psalms
  see *Symphonie de psaumes* (S35)

Symphony in three movements
  see *Symphony (1945)* (S47)

T. S. Eliot in memoriam
  see *Introitus* (14)

Tales for children
  see *Histoires pour enfants* (H8)

T1 *Tango, piano*
  Medium: Piano music
  Year: 1940
  Duration: 4'30"
  Published: (1) Mercury Music Corporation, 1941, plate
    no. 115-4, LC 72-229155; (2) B. Schott's Söhne, 1956
    (Edition Schott, 4917) plate no. BSS 39391

T2 *Tango, piano; orchestra*
  Medium: Orchestral music
  Year: 1953
  Duration: 3'
  First performance: Los Angeles; Evenings on the Roof;
    Robert Craft, conductor; 18 October 1953
  Published: (1) Mercury Music Corporation, 1954,
    LC M55-2224; (2) B. Schott's Söhne, 1956 (Edition
    Schott, 4569) plate no. BSS 39392

T3 *Tango, piano; arr., orchestra*
  Medium: Orchestral music
  Notes: Arranged by Felix Guenther
  First performance: Robin Hood Dell; Benny Goodman,
    conductor; July 1941

T4 *Tango, piano; arr., 2 pianos*
  Medium: Piano music (2 pianos)
  Notes: Arranged by Victor Babin
  Published: (1) B. Schott's Söhne, 1964 (Edition Schott,
    4720) plate no. BSS 40861; (2) Mercury Music
    Corporation, 1962

T5 *Tango, piano; arr., violin & piano*
  Medium: Violin and piano music
  Notes: arranged by Samuel Dushkin; performance rights
    owned by Mercury Music Corporation

Published: (1) Associated Music Publishers, n.d.?,
disclaimed by the publishers

T6 *Threni*
Medium: Cantatas
Year: 1958
Alternate title: *Lamentationes Jeremiae prophetae*
Duration: 35'
Dedication: Norddeutscher Rundfunk
First performance: Venice; Igor Stravinsky, conductor;
23 September 1958
Published: (1) Boosey & Hawkes, 1958 (Hawkes pocket
scores, 709) plate no. B&H 18438; (2) Boosey & Hawkes,
1958, full score, LC M58-2062

T7 *Threni. Piano-vocal score*
Medium: Piano-vocal scores
Published: (1) Boosey & Hawkes, 1958, plate no. B&H
19445, LC M58-2061

Tilimbom
see *Histoires pour enfants. No. 1: Tilimbom; voice &
orchestra* (H10)

Tombeau de Claude Debussy
see *Symphonies d'instruments à vent* (S39)

Tourneys of rival tribes
see *Le sacre du printemps. Jeux des cités rivales; arr., piano*
(S7)

Unterschale
see *Russian peasant songs; women's voices, unaccompanied*
(R19)

Valse
see *L'histoire du soldat. Valse; arr., piano* (H7)

V1 *Valse des fleurs*
   Medium: Piano music (2 pianos)
   Year: 1914
   Notes: Manuscript lost in 1949

V2 *Valse pour les enfants*
   Medium: Piano music
   Year: 1917
   Alternate title: *A waltz for children*
   Published (1) Le Figaro, 21 May 1922 (reproduced in
      Stravinsky, the composer and his works, by Eric Walter
      White, p. 210)

V3 *Variations, orchestra*
   Medium: Orchestral music
   Year: 1964
   Alternate title: *Aldous Huxley in memoriam*
   Duration: 5′
   Dedication: Aldous Huxley
   First performance: Chicago; Robert Craft, conductor;
      17 April 1965
   Published: (1) Boosey & Hawkes, 1965 (Hawkes pocket
      scores, 779) LC 68-41726/M; (2) Boosey & Hawkes,
      1965, full score, LC 66-43774/M

   Vesna sviashchennaia
   see *Le sacre du printemps* (S1)

   Von Himmel hoch
   see Z1

   Waltz
   see *Pièces faciles, piano, 4 hands (1915). No. 2: Waltz;
      instrumental septet* (P38)

   A waltz for children
   see *Valse pour les enfants* (V2)

The wedding
  see *Les noces* (N1)

W1 *Works, instrumental. Selections: Kamernye ansambli*
  Medium: Chamber-orchestra music; Wind octets;
    Concertos (String orchestra); String-orchestra music
  Contents: (1) Concerto, chamber orchestra, E♭ (C32);
    (2) Octet for winds (O1); (3) Concerto, string orchestra,
    D (C40)
  Published: (1) Muzyka, 1971

W2 *Works, instrumental. Selections: Sochineniia dlia fortepiano*
  Medium: Piano music (2 pianos)
  Alternate title: Sochineniia dlia fortepiano
  Contents: vol. 1 contents not determined; vol. 2: Concerto
    for piano and wind orchestra (see C34); Capriccio for
    piano and orchestra (see C7); Concerto for 2 pianos (see
    C38); Sonata for 2 pianos (see S24); Movements for
    piano and orchestra (see M13)
  Published: (1) Muzyka, n.d.?, LC 73-229592

W3 *Works, instrumental. Selections; arr., piano: Masterpieces
  for piano*
  Medium: Piano music
  Published: Marks Music Corporation, 1941

W4 *Works, piano, 4 hands. Selections; arr., band. A Stravinsky
  suite*
  Medium: Band music
  Alternate title: *A Stravinsky suite*
  Duration: 4'30"
  Notes: Arranged by Frank Erickson from *Pièces faciles* of
    1915 (see P36) and of 1917 (see P41)
  Contents: (1) March; (2) Andante; (3) Galop
  Published: (1) Chappell, 1968, LC 68-43769/M

Der Wüstling
  see *The rake's progress* (R3)

Zary-ptitsa
  see *L'oiseau de feu* (O8)

Zvedoliki
  see *Le roi des étoiles* (R11)

Zviedolikiĭ
  see *Le roi des étoiles* (R11)

Arrangements by Stravinsky

Z1 Bach, Johann Sebastian. *Einige canonische Veränderungen, organ, S.769; arr., mixed voices & orchestra*
    Medium: Choruses (Mixed voices) with orchestra
    Year: 1956
    Alternate title: *Von Himmel hoch da komm ich her*
    Published: (1) Boosey & Hawkes, 1956 (Hawkes pocket scores, 695) plate no. B&H 18284, LC M57-1347;
      (2) Boosey & Hawkes, 1956, full score, LC M57-663

Z2 Beethoven, Ludwig van. *Faust. Flohlied; arr., voice & orchestra*
    Medium: Songs with orchestra
    Year: 1910
    Alternate title: *Song of the flea*
    Published: (1) W. Bessel & Co.

Z3 Chaĭkovskiĭ, Petr Il'ich. *The sleeping beauty. Selections, arr., orchestra (1921)*
    Medium: Orchestral music
    Year: 1921

Z4 Chaĭkovskiĭ, Petr Il'ich. *The sleeping beauty. Selections; arr.,*
orchestra (1941)
Medium: Orchestral music
Year: 1941
Duration: 6'
Contents: (1) Pas de deux: Adagio, Variation I, Variation II,
Coda
Published: (1) B. Schott's Söhne, 1953 (Edition Schott,
4409) plate no. BSS 37500a; (2) Associated Music
Publishers, 1953 (Edition Schott, 4409)

Z5 *Chant des bateliers du Volga; arr., winds & percussion*
Medium: Band music
Year: 1917
Alternate title: (1) *Song of the Volga boatmen;* (2) *Hymne*
à la nouvelle Russie
Published: (1) J. & W. Chester, 1923, 1920, plate no. JWC
18; (2) Autograph Editions, 1970, includes score and parts

Z6 Chopin, Fryderyk Franciszek. *Nocturne, piano, op. 31, no. 2,*
A-flat major; arr., orchestra
Medium: Orchestral music
Year: 1909

Z7 Chopin, Fryderyk Franciszek. *Valse brillante, piano, E-flat*
major; arr., orchestra
Medium: Orchestral music
Year: 1909
Notes: Based on Chopin's op. 18 (1831) or a waltz in the
same key without opus number (1827)

Z8 Gesualdo, Carlo, principe di Venosa. *Sacrae cantiones, 6-7*
voices. Selections; arr., chorus
Medium: Choruses (Mixed voices), Unaccompanied

Year: 1957

Contents: (1) Da pacem Domine; (2) Assumpta est Maria; (3) Illumina nos

Published: (1) Boosey & Hawkes, 1960, plate no. 18690, LC M60-2176; (2) Boosey & Hawkes, 1957 (Hawkes pocket scores, 725) contains Illumina nos only, LC M58-228

Z9 Grieg, Edvard Hagerup. *Kobald; arr., orchestra*

Medium: Orchestral music

Year: 1909

Z10 Lisle, Claude Joseph Rouget de. *La marseillaise; arr., violin*

Medium: Violin music

Year: 1919

Z11 Musorgskiĭ, Modest Petrovich. *Boris Godunov. Prologue; arr., piano*

Medium: Piano music

Year: 1918

Z12 Musorgskiĭ, Modest Petrovich. *Khovanshchina, Selections; piano-vocal score*

Medium: Piano-vocal scores

Year: 1913

Published: (1) W. Bessel & Co., 1914, plate no. 7396, contains piano-vocal score of final chorus only

Z13 Musorgskiĭ, Modest Petrovich. *Pesnia o blokhe; arr., voice & orchestra*

Medium: Songs with orchestra

Year: 1910

Published: (1) W. Bessel & Co., n.d.?, plate no. 7320; (2) Boosey & Hawkes, n.d.?; (3) Muzyka, 1970

Z14 Sibelius, Jean. *Canzonetta, string orchestra, op. 62a; arr., instrumental octet*
   Medium: Octets
   Year: 1963
   Published: (1) Breitkopf und Härtel, 1964 (Partitur-Bibliothek, 3888) LC 64-53324/M

Z15 Smith, John Stafford, supposed composer. *The star-spangled banner; arr., orchestra*
   Medium: Orchestral music; Choruses (Mixed voices) with orchestra
   Year: 1941
   Notes: Choral part is optional
   Published: (1) Mercury Music Corporation, 1941, LC 65-77927/M

Z16 Smith, John Stafford, supposed composer. *The star-spangled banner; arr., orchestra. Piano-vocal score*
   Medium: Piano-vocal scores
   Published: (1) Mercury Music Corporation, 1941, LC 65-77926/M

Z17 Smith, John Stafford, supposed composer. *The star-spangled banner; arr., orchestra; arr., band*
   Medium: Band music
   Year: 1942
   Notes: Arranged by Charles Cushing in 1942

Z18 Wolf, Hugo. *Spanisches Liederbuch. Selections; arr., voice & instrumental ensemble*
   Medium: Songs with instrumental ensemble
   Year: 1968
   Contents: (1) Herr, was trägt der Boden hier; (2) Wunden trägst du
   Published: (1) Boosey & Hawkes, 1969, LC 76-222226

Indexes

A PRELIMINARY NOTE. The relationship of the two world wars to Stravinsky's residence and to the Berne Copyright Convention (which neither the United States nor Russia had signed) has a direct bearing on the complexities of the composer and his publishers.

Prior to the start of the First World War, it had first appeared that Stravinsky's publisher might be Jurgenson, of Moscow. The conductor Alexandre Siloti, who had premiered both *Feu d'artifice* and the *Scherzo fantastique* at a St. Petersburg concert in 1909, called the attention of Schott to the young composer that year, but the time was not ready for full development of the Stravinsky-Schott relationship; Diaghilev's ballet productions for Paris took the composer to France and marked the tentative start of Stravinsky's association with Serge Koussevitsky's Edition Russe de Musique.

The outbreak of the war ended the publication of new works by German firms for many years, and Stravinsky found it more convenient to employ the services of Henn in Switzerland (where he was residing) and Chester. In 1920, when he returned to France, he returned to the Edition Russe de Musique and granted this firm the publication rights to almost every new composition until 1931, after which several major works were given to Schott.

In 1939, the start of the Second World War encouraged Stravinsky to move to the United States. These years saw the publication of his works by Mercury, and Chappell, but particularly Associated Music Publishers. The latter was allied with Schott, happily enough for the composer.

Right at the end of 1945, Stravinsky became an American citizen and was approached by Boosey & Hawkes with publication arrangements that proved satisfactory for the remainder of the composer's life.

The first work of his to be published in his native land after the Revolution was *Petroushka*, issued in 1962 by Gosudarstvennyi Muzkal'noe izd-vo. This was followed in later years by other editions of works regarded as being in public domain, which was a consideration both financially and stylistically satisfactory to the Soviet house.

1. Publisher index

Abby Music Co. (609 Fifth Avenue, New York, 10017)
P43 *Pièces faciles: Napolitana* (arr., wind sextet)

Associated Music Publishers, Inc. (609 Fifth Avenue, New York 10036; Belwin-Mills has replaced AMP as American agent for Schott; kindly verified by Barry O'Neal and Mrs. Geraldine Geber)
B1 *Babel*
B2 *Babel* (piano-vocal score)
C4 *Cantata* (piano-vocal score)
C11 *The card party*
C12 *The card party* (piano reduction)
C23 *Circus polka*
C24 *Circus polka* (orchestral version)
C25 *Circus polka* (arr., band)
C26 *Circus polka* (arr., 2 pianos)
C27 *Circus polka* (arr., violin & piano)
C32 *Concerto, chamber orchestra, E flat* ("Dumbarton Oaks")
C33 *Concerto, chamber orchestra, E flat* (2 piano version)
C38 *Concerto, 2 pianos*
C41 *Concerto, violin, D major*
C42 *Concerto, violin, D major* (violin & piano version)
D1 *Danses concertantes*
D2 *Danses concertantes* (arr., 2 pianos)

E3 *Elegie, viola*
E12 *Etudes, piano*
F4 *Feu d'artifice*
N3 *Norwegian moods*
O4 *Ode*
O14 *L'oiseau de feu: Berceuse* (violin & piano version)
O15 *L'oiseau de feu: Berceuse* (violin & piano version, 1932)
O18 *L'oiseau de feu: Berceuse* (arr., piano)
O32 *L'oiseau de feu: La ronde* (arr., chorus & piano)
O33 *L'oiseau de feu: Scherzo* (violin & piano version)
O37 *L'oiseau de feu: Selections* (arr., piano)
P1 *Pastorale*
P2 *Pastorale* (violin & winds version)
P4 *Pastorale* (violin & piano version)
S6 *Le sacre du printemps: Danse sacrale*
S9 *Scènes de ballet*
S12 *Scherzo à la russe* (orchestral version)
S13 *Scherzo à la russe* (piano version)
S14 *Scherzo à la russe* (2 piano version)
S15 *Scherzo fantastique*
S24 *Sonata, 2 pianos*
S43 *Symphony, C*
S47 *Symphony (1945)*
T5 *Tango* (arr., violin & piano)
Z4 *Chaĭkovskiĭ: Sleeping beauty: Selections* (arr., orchestra)

Autograph Editions (400 Madison Avenue, New York, 10036)
Z5 *Chant des bateliers du Volga* (arr., winds & percussion)

BMI
O35 *L'oiseau de feu: Selections* (arr., orchestra)

Belaieff, M. P. (c/o C. F. Peters Corporation, 373 Park Avenue South, New York, 10016)
F2 *Le faune et la bergère*
F3 *Le faune et la bergère* (voice & piano version)

Belwin-Mills Publishing Co. (Melville, L. I., New York, 11746)
O35 *L'oiseau de feu: Selections* (arr., orchestra)

Benjamin, Anton J. (Dorotheenstrasse 176, Hamburg 39; not verified by publisher)
E12 *Etudes, piano, op. 7*

Bessel & Co., W. (78 rue de Monceau, Paris 8; not verified by publisher)
    Z2 *Beethoven: Faust: Flohlied* (arr., voice & orchestra)
    Z12 *Musorgskiĭ: Khovanshchina: Selections* (piano-vocal score)
    Z13 *Musorgskiĭ: Pesnie o blokhe* (arr., voice & orchestra)

Boosey & Hawkes (30 West 57 Street, New York, 10019; Oceanside, New York, 11572; partial verification by John Bice and Sylvia Goldstein; full verification prevented by a plant and warehouse fire in the 1950's)
    A1 *Abraham and Isaac*
    A2 *Abraham and Isaac* (piano-vocal score)
    A3 *Agon*
    A4 *Agon* (2 piano version)
    A7 *Apollon musagète* (1947 version)
    A8 *Ave Maria*
    A9 *Ave Maria* (1949 version)
    B5 *Le baiser de la fée* (1950 version)
    B6 *Le baiser de la fée* (piano version, 1950)
    B7 *Le baiser de la fée (Suite)*
    B8 *Le baiser de la fée (Suite)* (violin & piano version)
    B9 *Le baiser de la fée (Suite)* (1949 version)
    B11 *Le baiser de la fée: Deuxième tableau: Selection* (violin & piano version)
    C0.5 *Canon, orchestra*
    C1 *Canon on a Russian popular theme*
    C3 *Cantata*
    C4 *Cantata* (piano-vocal score)
    C5 *Canticum sacrum*
    C6 *Canticum sacrum* (piano-vocal score)
    C9 *Capriccio* (1949 version)
    C10 *Capriccio* (2 piano version)
    C13 *Le chant du rossignol*
    C14 *Le chant du rossignol* (piano version)
    C16 *Le chant du rossignol: Selections* (violin & piano version)
    C35 *Concerto, piano & band* (1950 version)
    C36 *Concerto, piano & band* (2 piano version)
    C39 *Concerto, string orchestra, D* ("Basle concerto")
    C40 *Concerto, string orchestra, D* (1946 version)
    C43 *Credo*
    C44 *Credo* (1949 version)
    C45 *Credo* (1964 version)
    D4 *Double canon*
    D5 *The dove descending breaks the air*
    E5 *Elegy for J. F. K.*

P23 *Petroushka: Danse russe* (violin & piano version)
P28 *Petroushka: Fête populaire* (arr., piano)
P29 *Petroushka: Selections* (piano version)
P32 *Petroushka: Selections* (arr., 2 pianos)
P35 *Pièces, string quartet*
P45 *Poèmes de Verlaine, op. 9*
P46 *Poèmes de Verlaine* (1953 version)
P47 *Poèmes de Verlaine* (voice & orchestra version)
P49 *Poems of Balmont* (1947 version)
P50 *Poems of Balmont* (voice & chamber orchestra version)
P51 *Poésie de la lyrique japonaise*
P52 *Poésie de la lyrique japonaise* (voice & chamber orchestra version)
P53 *Praeludium, jazz ensemble*
P58 *Pulcinella*
P59 *Pulcinella* (1965 version)
P61 *Pulcinella (Suite)*
P62 *Pulcinella (Suite)* (1947 version)
P63 *Pulcinella (Suite)* (1949 version)
P66 *Pulcinella: Selections* (violin & piano version)
R3 *The rake's progress*
R4 *The rake's progress: Libretto*
R5 *The rake's progress* (piano-vocal score)
R6 *The rake's progress: Lullaby* (2 recorder version)
R7 *Renard*
R9 *Requiem canticles*
R10 *Requiem canticles* (piano-vocal score)
R13 *Le rossignol*
R14 *Le rossignol* (1962 version)
R15 *Le rossignol* (piano-vocal score)
S1 *Le sacre du printemps*
S17 *Septet*
S18 *Septet* (2 piano version)
S19 *Serenade, piano, A*
S20 *A sermon, a narrative and a prayer*
S21 *A sermon, a narrative and a prayer* (piano-vocal score)
S23 *Sonata, piano (1924)*
S26 *Songs from William Shakespeare*
S27 *Songs from William Shakespeare* (voice & piano version)
S32 *Suite, violin & piano*
S33 *Suite italienne, violin & piano*
S34 *Suite italienne, violoncello & piano*
S35 *Symphonie de psaumes*
S37 *Symphonie de psaumes* (1948 version)

S38 *Symphonie de psaumes* (piano-vocal score, 1948 version)
S40 *Symphonie d'instruments à vent* (1947 version)
S45 *Symphony, E-flat major, op. 1* (1914 version)
T6 *Threni*
T7 *Threni* (piano-vocal score)
V3 *Variations, orchestra*
Z1 *Bach: Von Himmel hoch* (arr., chorus & orchestra)
Z8 *Gesualdo: Sacrae cantiones* (arr., chorus)
Z13 *Musorgskiĭ: Pesnia o blokhe* (arr., voice & orchestra)
Z18 *Wolf: Spanisches Liederbuch: Selections* (arr., voice & instrumental ensemble)

Boston Music Co. (116 Boylston Street, Boston, 02116; not verified by publisher)
O18 *L'oiseau de feu: Berceuse* (arr., piano)

Breitkopf und Härtel (Walkmühlstrasse 52, Postfach 74, Wiesbaden; kindly verified by Bettian Pauck; items P21 and P22 were issued by Breitkopf und Härtel in New York only)
P15 *Petroushka*
P21 *Petroushka: Danse de la ballerine* (arr., chorus, violin & piano)
P22 *Petroushka: Danse des cochers* (arr., chorus & piano)
Z14 *Sibelius: Canzonetta* (arr., instrumental octet)

Broude Brothers (56 West 45 Street, New York, 10036; not verified by publisher)
O8 *L'oiseau de feu*
O12 *L'oiseau de feu (Suite)* (1945 version)

Chappell & Co., Inc. (609 Fifth Avenue, New York, 10017; not verified by publisher)
E3 *Elegie, viola*
S11 *Scherzo à la russe* (jazz band version)
S12 *Scherzo à la russe* (orchestral version)
S24 *Sonata, 2 pianos*
W4 *Works, piano, 4 hands: A Stravinsky suite* (arr., band)

Charling Music Corporation (c/o Edwin H. Morris & Co., Inc., 31 West 54 Street, New York, 10019)
E1 *Ebony concerto*

Chester, J. & W. (Eagle Court, London E.C. 1; kindly verified by George Rizza and Faith Crook)
B13 *Berceuses du chat*
C18 *Chants russes*

C20 *Les cinq doigts*
C21 *Les cinq doigts* (arr., 2 guitars)
C21.5 *Les cinq doigts: No. 2: Allegro* (arr., guitar)
H1 *L'histoire du soldat*
H3 *L'histoire du soldat* (piano-vocal score)
H4 *L'histoire du soldat (Suite)*
H5 *L'histoire du soldat (Suite)* (piano, clarinet & violon version)
H7 *L'histoire du soldat: Valse* (arr., piano)
H8 *Histoires pour enfants*
I3 *Instrumental miniatures*
N1 *Les noces*
N2 *Les noces* (piano-vocal score)
O11 *L'oiseau de feu (Suite)* (1919 version)
O27 *L'oiseau de feu: La ronde* (arr., organ)
O36 *L'oiseau de feu: Selections* (arr., organ)
P1 *Pastorale*
P33 *Piano-rag music*
P34 *Pieces, clarinet*
P36 *Pièces faciles, piano, 4 hands (1915)*
P41 *Pièces faciles, piano, 4 hands (1917)*
P56 *Pribaoutki*
P57 *Pribaoutki* (voice & piano version)
P60 *Pulcinella* (piano version)
P63.5 *Pulcinella: Con queste paroline* (voice & piano version)
P64 *Pulcinella: Gavotta con variazioni* (piano version)
P65 *Pulcinella: Scherzino* (piano version)
R1 *Ragtime*
R2 *Ragtime* (piano version)
R7 *Renard*
R8 *Renard* (piano-vocal score)
R12 *Le roi des étoiles* (piano-vocal score)
R19 *Russian peasant songs*
R20 *Russian peasant songs* (women's voice & 4 horns version)
S25 *Songs (1954)*
S30 *Suite, orchestra, no. 1*
S31 *Suite, orchestra, no. 2*
Z5 *Chant des bateliers du Volga* (arr., winds & percussion)

Edition Musicus (333 West 52 Street, New York, 10019; not verified by publisher)
O17 *L'oiseau de feu: Berceuse* (arr., bassoon & piano)
O19 *L'oiseau de feu: Berceuse* (arr., string orchestra)
O20 *L'oiseau de feu: Berceuse* (arr., violin & piano)

O21 *L'oiseau de feu: Berceuse* (arr., violoncello & piano)
O25 *L'oiseau de feu: La ronde* (arr., oboe, bassoon & piano)
O26 *L'oiseau de feu: La ronde* (arr., oboe, clarinet & piano)
O29 *L'oiseau de feu: La ronde* (arr., viola & piano)
O30 *L'oiseau de feu: La ronde* (arr., violin, viola & piano)
P5 *Pastorale (arr.,* flute & piano)
P18 *Petroushka* (arr., orchestra)

Edition Russe de Musique (c/o Boosey & Hawkes, 30 West 57 Street, New
York, 10019; not verified by the publisher)
A5 *Apollon musagète*
A6 *Apollon musagète* (piano version)
A7 *Apollon musagète* (1947 version)
A8 *Ave Maria*
B3 *Le baiser de la fée*
B4 *Le baiser de la fée* (piano version)
B5 *Le baiser de la fée* (1950 version)
B7 *Le baiser de la fée (Suite)*
B8 *Le baiser de la fée (Suite)* (violin & piano version)
B10 *Le baiser de la fée: Deuxième tableau: Selection* (violin & piano
version)
C7 *Capriccio*
C8 *Capriccio* (2 piano version)
C13 *Le chant du rossignol*
C14 *Le chant du rossignol* (piano version)
C16 *Le chant du rossignol: Selections* (violin & piano version)
C34 *Concerto, piano & band*
C36 *Concerto, piano & band* (2 pianos)
C43 *Credo*
D7 *Duo concertante*
E8 *Etudes, orchestra*
M3 *Mavra*
M4 *Mavra* (piano-vocal score)
M5 *Mavra: Drug moĭ milyĭ* (violin & piano version)
M6 *Mavra: Drug moĭ milyĭ* (violoncello & piano version)
M7 *Mavra: Drug moĭ milyĭ* (voice & piano version)
O1 *Octet, winds*
O3 *Octet, winds* (arr., piano)
O5 *Oedipus rex*
O7 *Oedipus rex* (piano-vocal score)
P7 *Pater noster*
P9 *Perséphone*
P10 *Perséphone* (1949 version)

P11 *Perséphone* (piano-vocal score)
P13 *Petites chansons*
P14 *Petites chansons* (voice & orchestra version)
P15 *Petroushka*
P16 *Petroushka* (1947 version)
P17 *Petroushka* (piano 4-hand version, 1947)
P18 *Petroushka* (arr., orchestra)
P23 *Petroushka: Danse russe* (violin & piano version)
P29 *Petroushka: Selections* (piano version)
P31 *Petroushka: Selections* (arr., piano)
P32 *Petroushka: Selections* (arr., 2 pianos)
P35 *Pièces, string quartet*
P48 *Poems of Balmont*
P49 *Poems of Balmont* (1947 version)
P51 *Poésie de la lyrique japonaise*
P52 *Poésie de la lyrique japonaise* (voice & chamber orchestra version)
P58 *Pulcinella*
P61 *Pulcinella (Suite)*
P63 *Pulcinella (Suite)* (1949 version)
R13 *Le rossignol*
R15 *Le rossignol* (piano-vocal score)
R17 *Le rossignol: Marche chinoise* (arr., piano)
R18 *Le rossignol: Selections* (piano-vocal score)
S1 *Le sacre du printemps*
S3 *Le sacre du printemps* (piano 4-hand version)
S19 *Serenade, piano, A*
S23 *Sonata, piano (1924)*
S32 *Suite, violin & piano*
S33 *Suite italienne, violin & piano*
S34 *Suite italienne, violoncello & piano*
S35 *Symphonie de psaumes*
S36 *Symphonie de psaumes* (piano-vocal score)
S38 *Symphonie de psaumes* (piano-vocal score, 1948 version)
S41 *Symphonie d'instruments à vent* (arr., piano)

Edition de la Sirène (c/o La Sirène de Paris, 20 rue Oareau, Paris 14; not
   verified by publisher)
   R1 *Ragtime*
   R2 *Ragtime* (piano version)

Eulenberg Ltd., Ernst (c/o Schott Music Publishers, Brunswick Road,
   Ashford, Kent, England; kindly verified by Julian Hamlet)
   S47 *Symphony (1945)*

Feuilles musicales et courrier suisse du disque (Case 30, Lausanne 19; not verified by publisher)
    P12 *Petit ramusianum harmonique*
    P39 *Pièces faciles, piano, 4 hands (1915): Polka* (cimbalom version)

Le Figaro (40 dr. pt. Champs-Elysées, Paris 8; not verified by publisher)
    V2 *Valse pour les enfants*

Forberg, Robert (Mirbachstrasse 7, 53 Bonn/Bad Godesberg)
    P3 *Pastorale* (soprano & wind version)
    R11 *Le roi des étoiles*
    R12 *Le roi des étoiles* (piano-vocal score)
    S45 *Symphony, E-flat major, op. 1* (1914 version)
    S46 *Symphony, E-flat major, op. 1* (arr., piano, 4 hands)

Galaxy Music (2121 Broadway, New York, 10023)
    O22 *L'oiseau de feu: Berceuse* (arr., chorus & piano)

Gosudarstvennyi Muzykal'noe izd-vo (c/o MCA Music, 445 Park Avenue, New York, 10022; not verified by publisher)
    B8 *Le baiser de la fée (Suite)* (violin & piano version)
    O8 *L'oiseau de feu*
    P4 *Pastorale* (violin & piano version)
    P15 *Petroushka*
    P23 *Petroushka: Danse russe* (violin & piano version)
    P29 *Petroushka: Selections* (piano version)
    S46 *Symphony, E-flat major, op. 1* (arr., piano, 4 hands)

Gray Co., Inc., H. W. (159 East 48 Street, New York, 10017)
    O27 *L'oiseau de feu: La ronde* (arr., organ)

Hansen Music & Books, Charles (1842 West Avenue, Miami Beach, Florida, 33139; not verified by publisher)
    E1 *Ebony concerto*
    E2 *Ebony concerto* (arr., clarinet & band)

Hansen, Wilhelm (Gothersgade 9-11, København K; kindly verified by Hanne Wilhelm Hansen)
    C28 *Concertino, string quartet*
    C29 *Concertino, string quartet* (4-hand piano version)
    C30 *Concertino, string quartet* (winds & string version)
    C31 *Concertino, string quartet* (arr., piano)

Henn, Ad. (8 rue de Hesse, Genève; not verified by publisher)
    B13 *Berceuses du chat*
    B14 *Berceuses du chat* (voice & piano version)

P36 *Pièces faciles, piano, 4 hands (1915)*
P41 *Pièces faciles, piano, 4 hands (1917)*
P56 *Pribaoutki*
P57 *Pribaoutki* (voice & piano version)
R7 *Renard*
R8 *Renard* (piano-vocal score)

Homeyer & Co., Charles (156 Boylston Street, Boston, 02116; not verified by publisher)
    O18 *L'oiseau de feu: Berceuse* (arr., piano)

International Music Co. (509 Fifth Avenue, New York, 10017; not verified by publisher)
    E12 *Etudes, piano, op. 7*
    H1 *L'histoire du soldat*
    F4 *Feu d'artifice*
    H5 *L'histoire du soldat (Suite)* (piano, clarinet & violin version)
    S38 *Symphonie de psaumes* (piano-vocal score, 1948 version)

Jurgenson, A. (c/o MCA Music, 445 Park Avenue, New York, 10022; now owned by Gosudarstvennyi Muzykal'noe izd-vo; not verified by publisher; c/o Robert Forberg Musikverlag, Mirbachstrasse 7, 53 Bonn/Bad Godesberg, which firm provided verifications)
    E12 *Etudes, piano, op. 7*
    M11 *Mélodies, op. 6*
    O8 *L'oiseau de feu*
    O9 *L'oiseau de feu* (piano version)
    O10 *L'oiseau de feu (Suite)*
    O13 *L'oiseau de feu: Berceuse* (revised)
    P1 *Pastorale*
    P45 *Poèmes de Verlaine*
    R11 *Le roi des étoiles*
    S15 *Scherzo fantastique*
    S16 *Scherzo fantastique* (arr., piano)
    S45 *Symphony, E-flat major, op. 1* (1914 version)

Kalmus, Edwin F. (P. O. Box 1007, Commack, New York, 11725)
    H1 *L'histoire du soldat*
    H2 *L'histoire du soldat* (libretto)
    O11 *L'oiseau de feu (Suite)* (1919 version)
    P15 *Petroushka*
    S1 *Le sacre du printemps*
    S45 *Symphony, E-flat major, op. 1* (1914 version)

Leeds Music Corporation (c/o MCA Music, 445 Park Avenue, New York, 10022; not verified by publisher)
    O12 *L'oiseau de feu (Suite)* (1945 version)
    O31 *L'oiseau de feu: La ronde* (arr., voice & piano)

Macmillan & Co. (866 Third Avenue, New York, 10022; not verified by publisher)
    S28 *Souvenir d'une marche boche*

Marks Music Corporation, Edward B. (136 West 52 Street, New York, 10019; kindly verified by Don Malin)
    C15 *Le chant du rossignol: Marche chinoise* (arr., piano)
    E13 *Etudes, piano, op. 7: No. 4*
    H6 *L'histoire du soldat: Devil's dance* (arr., piano)
    O23 *L'oiseau de feu: Danse infernale* (arr., piano)
    O24 *L'oiseau de feu: La ronde* (piano version)
    O37 *L'oiseau de feu: Selections* (arr., piano)
    O38 *L'oiseau de feu: Supplications* (arr., piano)
    O39 *L'oiseau de feu: Supplications* (arr., violin & piano)
    P6 *Pastorale* (arr., piano)
    P20 *Petroushka: Chez Petroushka* (arr., piano)
    P24 *Petroushka: Danse russe* (arr., piano)
    P25 *Petroushka: Danse russe* (arr., piano, 4 hands)
    P26 *Petroushka: Danse russe* (arr., 2 pianos)
    P28 *Petroushka: Fête populaire* (arr., piano)
    P42 *Pièces faciles, piano, 4 hands (1915): Napolitana* (arr., piano)
    R16 *Le rossignol: Chant du rossignol* (arr., piano)
    R19 *Russian peasant's songs*
    S4 *Le sacre du printemps: Les augures printaniers* (arr., piano)
    S5 *Le sacre du printemps: Danse des adolescents* (arr., piano)
    S7 *Le sacre du printemps: Jeux des cités rivales* (arr., piano)
    S8 *Le sacre du printemps: Ronde printanière* (arr., piano)
    W3 *Works, instrumental: Selections: Masterpieces for piano* (arr., piano)

Mayfair Music Corporation (c/o Edwin F. Morris & Co., Inc., 31 West 54 Street, New York, 10019)
    E1 *Ebony concerto*

Mercury Music Corporation (c/o Theodore Presser, Presser Place, Bryn Mawr, Pennsylvania, 19010)
    P34 *Pieces, clarinet*
    T1 *Tango, piano*
    T2 *Tango, piano* (orchestral version)
    T4 *Tango, piano* (arr., 2 pianos)

T5 *Tango, piano* (arr., violin & piano)
Z15 *Smith: The star-spangled banner* (arr., orchestra)
Z16 *Smith: The star-spangled banner* (piano-vocal score)

Morris & Co., Inc., Edwin H. (31 West 54 Street, New York, 10019; kindly
verified by Charlotte Day State)
E1 *Ebony concerto*
E2 *Ebony concerto* (arr., clarinet & band)

Muzyka (c/o MCA Music, 445 Park Avenue, New York, 10022; not
verified by publisher)
A3 *Agon*
B11 *Le baiser de la fée: Deuxième tableau: Selection* (violin & piano
version)
C28 *Concertino, string quartet*
C42 *Concerto, violin, D major* (violin & piano version)
O40 *Orpheus*
P19 *Petroushka* (arr., piano)
P35 *Pièces, string quartet*
P44 *Pièces faciles, piano, 4 hands (1917): Selections* (chamber
orchestra version)
S1 *Le sacre du printemps*
S3 *Le sacre du printemps; piano, 4 hands*
S29 *Suites, orchestra*
S34 *Suite italienne, violoncello & piano*
S35 *Symphonie de psaumes*
W1 *Works, instrumental: Selections: Kamernye ansambli*
W2 *Works, instrumental: Selections: Sochineniia dlia fortepiano*
Z13 *Musorgskiĭ: Pesnia o blokhe* (arr., voice & orchestra)

Norton & Co., Inc., W. W. (55 Fifth Avenue, New York, 10003; kindly
verified by David Hamilton)
P15 *Petroushka*

Organ Music Co. (not verified by publisher)
O27 *L'oiseau de feu: La ronde* (arr., organ)

Peters Corporation, C. F. (373 Park Avenue South, New York, 10016)
S45 *Symphony, E-flat major, op. 1* (1914 version)

Porchet & Cie., V. (not verified by publisher)
P12 *Petit ramunsianum harmonique*

La Revue Musicale (Editions Richard-Masse, 7 place St.-Sulpice, Paris 6;
not verified by publisher)
S42 *Symphonies d'instruments à vent: Finale* (piano version)

Russischer Musik-Verlag
  see Edition Russe de Musique

Schott Music Publishers (Brunswick Road, Ashford, Kent, England; kindly
  verified by Julian Hamlet)
  C26 *Circus polka* (arr., 2 pianos)
  S14 *Scherzo à la russe* (2 piano version)

Schott's Söhne, B. (Weihergarten 1-11, Postfach 3640, 36 Mainz; kindly
  verified by Heinz-Jürgen Hört and Jana Matejcek)
  B1 *Babel*
  B2 *Babel* (piano-vocal score)
  B13 *Berceuses du chat*
  B14 *Berceuses du chat* (voice & piano version)
  C4 *Cantata* (piano-vocal score)
  C11 *The card party*
  C12 *The card party* (piano version)
  C23 *Circus polka*
  C24 *Circus polka* (orchestral version)
  C27 *Circus polka* (arr., violin & piano)
  C32 *Concerto, chamber orchestra, E flat* ("Dumbarton Oaks")
  C33 *Concerto, chamber orchestra, E flat* (2 piano version)
  C38 *Concerto, 2 pianos*
  C41 *Concerto, violin, D major*
  C42 *Concerto, violin, D major* (violin & piano version)
  D1 *Danses concertantes*
  E3 *Elegie, viola*
  F4 *Feu d'artifice*
  F6 *Feu d'artifice* (arr., piano, 4 hands)
  H10 *Histoires pour enfants: Tilimbom* (voice & orchestra version)
  N3 *Norwegian moods*
  O4 *Ode*
  O8 *L'oiseau de feu*
  O9 *L'oiseau de feu* (piano version)
  O12 *L'oiseau de feu (Suite)* (1945 version)
  O13 *L'oiseau de feu: Berceuse* (revised)
  O14 *L'oiseau de feu: Berceuse* (violin & piano version)
  O15 *L'oiseau de feu: Berceuse* (violin & piano version, 1932)
  O28 *L'oiseau de feu: La ronde* (arr., piano)
  O32 *L'oiseau de feu: La ronde* (arr. chorus & piano)
  O33 *L'oiseau de feu: Scherzo* (violin & piano version)
  O37 *L'oiseau de feu: Selections* (arr., piano)
  P1 *Pastorale*
  P2 *Pastorale* (violin & winds version)

P3 *Pastorale* (soprano & winds version)
P4 *Pastorale* (violin & piano version)
P57 *Pribaoutki* (voice & piano version)
R1 *Ragtime*
R7 *Renard*
R8 *Renard* (piano-vocal score)
R19 *Russian peasant songs*
R20 *Russian peasant songs* (chorus & horns version)
S12 *Scherzo à la russe* (orchestral version)
S15 *Scherzo fantastique*
S24 *Sonata, 2 pianos*
S31 *Suite, orchestra, no. 2*
S43 *Symphony, C*
S47 *Symphony (1945)*
T1 *Tango*
T2 *Tango* (orchestral version)
T4 *Tango* (arr., 2 pianos)
Z4 *Chaĭkovskiĭ: The sleeping beauty: Selections* (arr., orchestra, 1941)

Sovetskiĭ Kompozitor (c/o MCA Music, 445 Park Avenue, New York,
10022; not verified by publisher)
P27 *Petroushka: Danse russe* (arr., 2 pianos, 8 hands)

Staff Music Publishing Co. (5640 Collins Avenue, Miami Beach, Florida,
33140)
O16 *L'oiseau de feu: Berceuse* (arr., band)
P30 *Petroushka: Selections* (arr., band)

Western International Music (2859 Holt Avenue, Los Angeles, California,
90034)
O27 *L'oiseau de feu: La ronde* (arr., organ)

Wiener Philharmonischer Verlag (Universal Edition, Wien; not verified
by the publisher)
P56 *Pribaoutki*
R1 *Ragtime*
R7 *Renard*
S30 *Suite, orchestra, no. 1*
S31 *Suite, orchestra, no. 2*

Unfinished, unpublished and/or lost compositions
B12 *Berceuse*
C2 *Canon, 2 horns*
C17 *Chant funèbre sur la morte de Rimsky-Korsakov, op. 5*
C19 *Church prayer*

C22 *Les cinq doigts. No. 8: Pesante, instrumental ensemble*
C37 *Concerto, piano & band. Largo; piano*
D3 *Dialogue between reason and joy*
E4 *Elegy, viola, unaccompanied; 2 violas*
E7 *Etude, piano*
F5 *Feu d'artifice, op. 4: piano*
L1 *Little canon*
M10 *Mavra. Selections; arr., jazz ensemble*
O34 *L'oiseau de feu. Selections; violin & piano*
P54 *Praeludium, jazz ensemble (1953)*
P55 *Praeludium, jazz ensemble; piano*
S22 *Sonata, piano (1904), F-sharp minor*
S36 *Symphonie de psaumes*
S39 *Symphonies d'instruments à vent*
S44 *Symphony, E-flat major, op. 1*
T3 *Tango, piano; arr., orchestra*
V1 *Valse des fleurs*
Z3 *Chaïkovskiï: The sleeping beauty: Selections; arr., orchestra (1921)*
Z6 *Chopin: Nocturne, piano, op. 32, no. 2, A-flat major; arr., orchestra*
Z7 *Chopin: Valse brillante, piano, E-flat major; arr., orchestra*
Z9 *Grieg: Kobald; arr., orchestra*
Z10 *Lisle: La marseillaise; arr., violin*
Z11 *Musorgskiï: Boris Godunov: Prologue; arr., piano*
Z17 *Smith: The star-spangled banner; arr., orchestra; arr., band*

2. Medium index

Ballets
A3 *Agon*
A5 *Apollon musagète*
A7 *Apollon musagète* (1947 version)
B3 *Le baiser de la fée*
B5 *Le baiser de la fée* (1950 version)
C11 *The card party*
N1 *Les noces*
O8 *L'oiseau de feu*
O40 *Orpheus*

P9 *Perséphone*
P10 *Perséphone* (1948 version)
P15 *Petroushka*
P16 *Petroushka* (1947 version)
P58 *Pulcinella*
P59 *Pulcinella* (1965 version)
S1 *Le sacre du printemps*
S9 *Scènes de ballet*

Band music
C17 *Chant funèbre sur la morte de Rimsky-Korsakov, op. 5*
C25 *Circus polka* (arr., band)
O16 *L'oiseau de feu: Berceuse* (arr., band)
P30 *Petroushka: Selections* (arr., band)
S39 *Symphonies d'instruments à vent*
S40 *Symphonies d'instruments à vent* (1947 version)
W4 *Works, piano, 4 hands: Selections* (arr., band)
Z5 *Chant des bateliers du Volga* (arr., winds & percussion)
Z17 *Smith: The star-spangled banner* (arr., band)

Bassoon and piano music
O17 *L'oiseau de feu: Berceuse* (arr., bassoon & piano)

Bassoon music (2 bassoons)
D6 *Duet, bassoons*

Cantatas
A1 *Abraham and Isaac*
B1 *Babel*
B2 *Babel* (piano-vocal score)
C3 *Cantata*
C4 *Cantata* (piano-vocal score)
C5 *Canticum sacrum*
C6 *Canticum sacrum* (piano-vocal score)
S20 *A sermon, a narrative and a prayer*
S35 *Symphonie de psaumes*
S36 *Symphonie de psaumes* (piano-vocal score)
S37 *Symphonie de psaumes* (1948 version)
S38 *Symphonie de psaumes* (piano-vocal score, 1948 version)
T6 *Threni*

Chamber orchestra music
C32 *Concerto, chamber orchestra, E flat*
D1 *Danses concertantes*

P44 *Pièces faciles, piano, 4 hands (1917): Selections* (chamber orchestra version)
W1 *Works, instrumental: Selections: Kamernye ansambli*

Choruses with orchestra
R9 *Requiem canticles*

Choruses (Men's voices) with instrumental ensemble
I4 *Introitus*

Choruses (Men's voices) with orchestra
B1 *Babel*
R11 *Le roi des étoiles*

Choruses (Men's voices) with piano
B2 *Babel*

Choruses (Mixed voices), Unaccompanied
A8 *Ave Marie*
A9 *Ave Maria* (1949 version)
C43 *Credo*
C44 *Credo* (1949 version)
C45 *Credo* (1964 version)
D5 *The dove descending breaks the air*
P7 *Pater noster*
P8 *Pater noster* (1949 version)
Z8 *Gesualdo: Sacrae cantiones: Selections* (arr., chorus)

Choruses (Mixed voices) with instrumental ensemble
N1 *Les noces*

Choruses (Mixed voices) with orchestra
P9 *Perséphone*
P10 *Perséphone* (1949 version)
Z1 *Bach: Von Himmel hoch* (arr., chorus & orchestra)
Z15 *Smith: The star-spangled banner* (arr., chorus & orchestra)

Choruses (Mixed voices) with winds
M1 *Mass*

Choruses (Women's voices), Unaccompanied
R19 *Russian peasant songs*

Choruses (Women's voices) with 4 horns
R20 *Russian peasant songs* (women's voices & 4 horns version)

Choruses (Women's voices) with piano
> O32 *L'oiseau de feu: La ronde* (arr., women's voices & piano)
> P22 *Petroushka: Danse des cochers* (arr., women's voices & piano)

Choruses (Women's voices) with piano and violin
> P21 *Petroushka: Danse de la ballerine* (arr., women's voices, violin & piano)

Cimbalom music
> P39 *Pièces faciles, piano, 4 hands (1915): Polka* (cimbalom version)

Clarinet music
> P34 *Pieces, clarinet*

Clarinet with band
> E2 *Ebony concerto* (arr., clarinet & band)

Clarinet with jazz ensemble
> E1 *Ebony concerto*

Concertos (Clarinet)
> E1 *Ebony concerto*
> E2 *Ebony concerto* (arr., clarinet & band)

Concertos (2 pianos)
> C38 *Concerto, 2 pianos*

Concertos (String orchestra)
> C39 *Concerto, string orchestra, D*
> C40 *Concerto, string orchestra, D* (revised)
> W1 *Works, instrumental: Selections: Kamernye ansambli*

Concertos (Violin)
> C41 *Concerto, violin, D major*

Flute and piano music
> P5 *Pastorale* (arr., flute & piano)

Guitar music
> C21.5 *Les cinq doigts: No. 2: Allegro* (arr., guitar)

Guitar music (2 guitars)
> C21 *Les cinq doigts* (arr., 2 guitars)

Horn music (2 horns)
> C2 *Canons, 2 horns*

Instrumental ensembles
  C22 *Les cinq doigts: Pesante* (instrumental ensemble version)
  C30 *Concertino, string quartet* (wind & strings version)
  I3 *Instrumental miniatures*
  P37 *Pièces faciles, piano, 4 hands (1915): March* (instrumental ensemble version)
  R1 *Ragtime*

Jazz ensembles
  M10 *Mavra: Selections* (arr., jazz ensemble)
  P53 *Praeludium, jazz ensemble*
  P54 *Praeludium, jazz ensemble* (1953 version)
  S11 *Scherzo à la russe*

Librettos
  H2 *L'histoire du soldat* (libretto)
  R4 *The rake's progress* (libretto)

Melodramas with instrumental septet
  H1 *L'histoire du soldat*

Octets
  Z14 *Sibelius: Canzonetta* (arr., instrumental octet)

Operas
  F7 *The flood*
  M3 *Mavra*
  O5 *Oedipus rex*
  O6 *Oedipus rex* (1948 version)
  R3 *The rake's progress*
  R7 *Renard*
  R13 *Le rossignol*
  R14 *Le rossignol* (1962 version)

Oratorios
  O5 *Oedipus rex*
  O6 *Oedipus rex* (1948 version)

Orchestral music
  A3 *Agon*
  B3 *Le baiser de la fée*
  B5 *Le baiser de la fée* (1950 version)
  B7 *Le baiser de la fée (Suite)*
  B9 *Le baiser de la fée (Suite, 1949)*
  C0.5 *Canon, orchestra*
  C1 *Canon on a Russian popular theme*

C13 *Le chant du rossignol*
C24 *Circus polka* (orchestral version)
E8 *Etudes, orchestra*
E9 *Etudes, orchestra* (1952 version)
F4 *Feu d'artifice*
G1 *Greeting prelude*
M12 *Monumentum pro Gesualdo de Venosa ad CD annum*
N3 *Norwegian moods*
O4 *Ode*
O8 *L'oiseau de feu*
O10 *L'oiseau de feu (Suite)*
O11 *L'oiseau de feu (Suite, 1919)*
O12 *L'oiseau de feu (Suite, 1945)*
O13 *L'oiseau de feu: Berceuse* (revised)
O35 *L'oiseau de feu: Selections* (arr., orchestra)
O40 *Orpheus*
P15 *Petroushka*
P16 *Petroushka* (1947 version)
P18 *Petroushka* (arr., orchestra)
P58 *Pulcinella*
P59 *Pulcinella* (1965 version)
P61 *Pulcinella (Suite)*
P62 *Pulcinella (Suite)* (1949 version)
P63 *Pulcinella (Suite)* (1947 version)
S1 *Le sacre du printemps*
S6 *Le sacre du printemps: Danse sacrale*
S9 *Scènes de ballet*
S12 *Scherzo à la russe* (orchestral version)
S15 *Scherzo fantastique*
S29 *Suites, orchestra, nos. 1 & 2*
S30 *Suite, orchestra, no. 1*
S31 *Suite, orchestra, no. 2*
T2 *Tango* (orchestral version)
T3 *Tango* (arr., orchestra)
V3 *Variations, orchestra*
Z3 *Chaĭkovskiĭ: The sleeping beauty: Selections* (arr., orchestra, 1921)
Z4 *Chaĭkovskiĭ: The sleeping beauty: Selections* (arr., orchestra, 1941)
Z6 *Chopin: Nocturne* (arr., orchestra)
Z7 *Chopin: Valse brillante* (arr., orchestra)
Z9 *Grieg: Kobald* (arr., orchestra)
Z15 *Smith: The star-spangled banner* (arr., orchestra)

Organ music

    E10 *Etudes, orchestra: Cantique* (arr., organ)
    O27 *L'oiseau de feu: La ronde* (arr., organ)
    O36 *L'oiseau de feu: Selections* (arr., organ)

Piano music

    A6 *Apollon musagète* (piano version)
    B4 *Le baiser de la fée* (piano version)
    B6 *Le baiser de la fée* (piano version, 1950)
    C12 *The card party* (piano version)
    C14 *Le chant du rossignol* (piano version)
    C15 *Le chant du rossignol: Marche chinoise* (arr., piano)
    C20 *Les cinq doigts*
    C23 *Circus polka*
    C31 *Concertino, string quartet* (arr., piano)
    C37 *Concerto, piano & band: Largo* (piano version)
    E7 *Etude, piano*
    E12 *Etudes, piano, op. 7*
    E13 *Etudes, piano, op. 7, no. 4*
    F5 *Feu d'artifice* (piano version)
    H6 *L'histoire du soldat: Devil's dance* (arr., piano)
    H7 *L'histoire du soldat: Valse* (arr., piano)
    H9 *Histoires pour enfants* (piano version)
    M9 *Mavra: Overture* (piano version)
    O3 *Octet, winds* (arr., piano)
    O9 *L'oiseau de feu* (piano version)
    O18 *L'oiseau de feu: Berceuse* (arr., piano)
    O23 *L'oiseau de feu: Danse infernale* (arr., piano)
    O24 *L'oiseau de feu: La ronde* (piano version)
    O28 *L'oiseau de feu: La ronde* (arr., piano)
    O37 *L'oiseau de feu: Selections* (arr., piano)
    O38 *L'oiseau de feu: Supplications* (arr., piano)
    O41 *Orpheus* (arr., piano)
    P6 *Pastorale* (arr., piano)
    P19 *Petroushka* (arr., piano)
    P20 *Petroushka: Chez Petroushka* (arr., piano)
    P24 *Petroushka: Danse russe* (arr., piano)
    P28 *Petroushka: Fête populaire* (arr., piano)
    P29 *Petroushka: Selections* (piano version)
    P31 *Petroushka: Selections* (arr., piano)
    P33 *Piano-rag music*
    P42 *Pièces faciles, piano, 4 hands (1915): Napolitana* (arr., piano)
    P55 *Praeludium, jazz ensemble* (piano version)

P60 *Pulcinella* (piano version)
P64 *Pulcinella: Gavotta con variazioni* (piano version)
P65 *Pulcinella: Scherzino* (piano version)
R2 *Ragtime* (piano version)
R16 *Le rossignol: Chant du rossignol* (arr., piano)
R17 *Le rossignol: Marche chinoise* (arr., piano)
S2 *Le sacre du printemps* (piano version)
S4 *Le sacre du printemps: Les augures printaniers* (arr., piano)
S5 *Le sacre du printemps: Danse des adolescents* (arr., piano)
S7 *Le sacre du printemps: Jeux des cités rivales* (arr., piano)
S8 *Le sacre du printemps: Ronde printanière* (arr., piano)
S10 *Scènes du ballet* (arr., piano)
S13 *Scherzo à la russe* (piano version)
S16 *Scherzo fantastique* (arr., piano)
S19 *Serenade, piano, A*
S22 *Sonata, piano (1904)*
S23 *Sonata, piano (1924)*
S28 *Souvenir d'une marche boche*
S41 *Symphonies d'instruments à vent* (arr., piano)
S42 *Symphonies d'instruments à vent: Finale* (piano version)
T1 *Tango*
V2 *Valse pour les enfants*
W3 *Works, instrumental: Selections* (arr., piano)
Z11 *Musorgskiĭ: Boris Godunov: Prologue* (arr., piano)

Piano music (2 pianos)
A4 *Agon* (2 piano version)
C8 *Capriccio, piano & orchestra* (2 piano version)
C10 *Capriccio, piano & orchestra* (2 piano version, 1949)
C26 *Circus polka* (arr., 2 pianos)
C33 *Concerto, chamber orchestra, E flat* (2 piano version)
C36 *Concerto, piano & band* (2 piano version)
C38 *Concerto, 2 pianos*
D2 *Danses concertantes* (arr., 2 pianos)
E11 *Etudes, orchestra: Madrid* (arr., 2 pianos)
M14 *Movements* (2 piano version)
P26 *Petroushka: Danse russe* (arr., 2 pianos)
P32 *Petroushka: Selections* (arr., 2 pianos)
S14 *Scherzo à la russe* (2 piano version)
S18 *Septet* (2 piano version)
S24 *Sonata, 2 pianos*
T4 *Tango* (arr., 2 pianos)
V1 *Valse des fleurs*
W2 *Works, instrumental: Selections: Sochineniia dlia fortepiano*

Piano music (2 pianos, 8 hands)
  P27 *Petroushka: Danse russe* (arr., 2 pianos, 8 hands)

Piano (4 hands)
  C29 *Concertino, string quartet* (4-hand piano version)
  F6 *Feu d'artifice* (arr., piano, 4 hands)
  P17 *Petroushka (1917)* (4-hand piano version)
  P25 *Petroushka: Danse russe* (arr., piano, 4 hands)
  P36 *Pièces faciles, piano, 4 hands (1915)*
  P41 *Pièces faciles, piano, 4 hands (1917)*
  S3 *Le sacre du printemps* (4-hand piano version)
  S46 *Symphony, E-flat major, op. 1* (arr., piano, 4 hands)

Piano-vocal scores (title citations below omit reference to this medium)
  A2 *Abraham and Isaac*
  B2 *Babel*
  C4 *Cantata*
  C6 *Canticum sacrum*
  F8 *The flood*
  H3 *L'histoire du soldat*
  M2 *Mass*
  M4 *Mavra*
  N2 *Les noces*
  O7 *Oedipus rex*
  P11 *Perséphone*
  R5 *The rake's progress*
  R8 *Renard*
  R10 *Requiem canticles*
  R12 *Le roi des étoiles*
  R15 *Le rossignol*
  R18 *Le rossignol: Selections*
  S21 *A sermon, a narrative and a prayer*
  S36 *Symphonie de psaumes*
  S38 *Symphonie de psaumes (1948 version)*
  T7 *Threni*
  Z12 *Musorgskiĭ: Boris Godunov: Khovanshchina: Selections*
  Z16 *Smith: The star-spangled banner*

Piano with band
  C34 *Concerto, piano & band*
  C35 *Concerto, piano & band (1950 version)*

Piano with orchestra
  C7 *Capriccio, piano & orchestra*

C9 *Capriccio, piano & orchestra* (1949 version)
M13 *Movements, piano & orchestra*

Quintets
P2 *Pastorale* (violin & wind version)

Recorder music (2 recorders)
R6 *The rake's progress: Lullaby* (2 recorder version)

Septets
H4 *L'histoire du soldat* (Suite)
P38 *Pièces faciles, piano, 4 hands (1915): Waltz* (septet version)
S17 *Septet, piano, winds & strings*

Songs, Unaccompanied
P12 *Petite ramusianum harmonique*

Songs with instrumental ensemble (see also Vocalises)
Z18 *Wolf: Spanisches Liederbuch: Selections* (arr., voice & instrumental ensemble)

Songs with orchestra
H10 *Histoires pour enfants: Tilimbom* (voice & orchestra version)
P14 *Petites chansons* (voice & orchestra version)
P47 *Poèmes de Verlaine, op. 9* (voice & orchestra version)
Z2 *Beethoven: Faust: Flohlied* (arr., voice & orchestra)
Z13 *Musorgskiĭ: Pesnia o blokhe* (arr., voice & orchestra)

Songs with piano (see also Vocalise)
B12 *Berceuse*
B14 *Berceuses du chat* (voice & piano version)
C18 *Chants russes*
I2 *In memoriam Dylan Thomas* (voice & piano version)
M7 *Mavra: Drug moĭ milyĭ* (voice & piano version)
M8 *Mavra: Net' ne zabyt'* (voice & piano version)
O31 *L'oiseau de feu: La ronde* (arr., voice & piano)
P13 *Petites chansons*
P57 *Pribaoutki* (voice & piano version)

Songs (High voice) with chamber orchestra
P50 *Poems of Balmont* (voice & chamber orchestra version)
P52 *Poésie de la lyrique japonaise* (voice & chamber orchestra version)

Songs (High voice) with flute, clarinet and viola
S26 *Songs from William Shakespeare*

Songs (High voice) with flute, harp and guitar
S25 *Songs (1954)*

Songs (High voice) with piano
P48 *Poems of Balmont*
P49 *Poems of Balmont (revised)*
P51 *Poésie de la lyrique japonaise*
S27 *Songs from William Shakespeare* (voice & piano version)

Songs (High voice) with string quartet and 4 trombones
I1 *In memoriam Dylan Thomas*

Songs (Low voice) with 3 clarinets
B13 *Berceuses du chat*

Songs (Low voice) with piano
M15 *The mushrooms going to war*
P63.5 *Pulcinella: Con queste paroline*

Songs (Medium voice) with chamber orchestra
A1 *Abraham and Isaac*
P56 *Pribaoutki*

Songs (Medium voice) with 3 clarinets
E5 *Elegy for J. F. K.*

Songs (Medium voice) with orchestra
F2 *La faune et la bergère*

Songs (Medium voice) with piano
A2 *Abraham and Isaac* (piano-vocal score)
F3 *Le faune et la bergère* (voice & piano version)
H8 *Histoires pour enfants*
M11 *Mélodies, op. 6*
O42 *The owl and the pussy cat*
P45 *Poèmes de Verlaine, op. 9*
P46 *Poèmes de Verlaine, op. 9* (1953 version)
S27 *Songs from William Shakespeare* (voice & piano version)

String-orchestra music
A5 *Apollon musagète*
A7 *Apollon musagète (1947 version)*
C39 *Concerto, string orchestra, D*
C40 *Concerto, string orchestra, D (revised)*
O19 *L'oiseau de feu: Berceuse* (arr., string orchestra)
W1 *Works, instrumental: Selections: Kamernye ansambli*

String quartets
    C28 *Concertino, string quartet*
    D4 *Double canon, string quartet*
    P35 *Pièces, string quartet*

Symphonies
    S35 *Symphonie de psaumes*
    S37 *Symphonie de psaumes* (1948 version)
    S43 *Symphony, C*
    S44 *Symphony, E-flat major, op. 1*
    S45 *Symphony, E-flat major, op. 1* (1914 version)
    S47 *Symphony (1945)*

Trios (Flute, clarinet, harp)
    E6 *Epitaphium*

Trios (Piano, clarinet, violin)
    H5 *L'histoire du soldat (Suite)*

Trios (Piano, oboe, bassoon)
    O25 *L'oiseau de feu: La ronde* (arr.)

Trios (Piano, oboe, clarinet)
    O26 *L'oiseau de feu: La ronde* (arr.)

Trios (Piano, viola, violin)
    O30 *L'oiseau de feu: La ronde* (arr., violin, viola & piano)

Trumpet music (2 trumpets)
    F1 *Fanfare for a new theatre*

Viola and piano music
    O29 *L'oiseau de feu: La ronde;* arr., viola & piano

Viola music
    E3 *Elegie, viola*

Viola music (2 violas)
    E4 *Elegie, viola* (2 viola version)

Violin music
    E3 *Elegie, viola*
    Z10 *Lisle: La marseillaise* (arr., violin)

Violin and piano music
    B8 *Le baiser de la fée (Suite)* (violin & piano version)
    B10 *Le baiser de la fée: Deuxième tableau: Selection* (violin & piano
        version, 1934)

B11 *Le baiser de la fée: Deuxième tableau: Selection* (violin & piano version, 1951)
C16 *Le chant du rossignol: Selections* (violin & piano version)
C27 *Circus polka* (arr., violin & piano)
C42 *Concerto, violin, D major* (violin & piano version)
D7 *Duo concertante*
M5 *Mavra: Drug moĭ milyĭ* (violin & piano version)
O14 *L'oiseau de feu: Berceuse* (violin & piano version)
O15 *L'oiseau de feu: Berceuse* (violin & piano version, 1932)
O20 *L'oiseau de feu: Berceuse* (arr., violin & piano)
O29 *L'oiseau de feu: La ronde* (arr., violin & piano)
O34 *L'oiseau de feu: Selections* (violin & piano version)
O39 *L'oiseau de feu: Supplications* (arr., violin & piano)
P4 *Pastorale* (violin & piano version)
P23 *Petroushka: Danse russe* (violin & piano version)
P66 *Pulcinella: Selections* (violin & piano version)
S32 *Suite italienne, violin & piano*
S33 *Suite italienne, violin & piano*
T5 *Tango* (arr., violin & piano)

Violin with orchestra
C41 *Concerto, violin, D major*

Violoncello and piano music
M6 *Mavra: Drug moĭ milyĭ* (violoncello & piano version)
O21 *L'oiseau de feu: Berceuse* (arr., violoncello & piano)
S34 *Suite italienne, violoncello & piano*

Vocal duets
L1 *Little canon*

Vocalises (Medium voice) with instrumental ensemble
P3 *Pastorale* (soprano & wind version)

Vocalises (Medium voice) with piano
P1 *Pastorale*

Wind octets
O1 *Octet, winds*
O2 *Octet, winds* (1952 version)
W1 *Works, instrumental: Selections: Kamernye ansambli*

Wind sextets (Flute, oboe, clarinets, bassoon, horn)
P43 *Pièces faciles, piano, 4 hands (1915): Napolitana* (arr., winds)

3. Index of proper names

Individuals and performing groups are listed here with an identification of their relationship to the works cited (arr.—arranger; comm.—commissioner; co-comp.—co-composer, or person whose music Stravinsky arranged; ded.—person or group to whom the work is dedicated; ed.—editor; perf.—performer; text—poet, librettist or scenarist; trans.—translator).

Abravanel, Maurice
    S9 *Scènes de ballet* (perf.)

Afanasiev, Alexander
    N1 *Les noces* (text)
    R19 *Russian peasant songs* (text)

Agosti, Guido
    O37 *L'oiseau de feu: Selections* (arr.)

Allegra, Edmond
    P34 *Pieces, clarinet* (perf.)

American ballet
    C11 *The card party* (perf.)

Anders, Ludwig
    B1 *Babel* (trans.)

Andersen, Hans Christian
    R13 *Le rossignol* (text)

André, Franz
    R11 *Le roi des étoiles* (perf.)

Ansermet, Ernest
    C7 *Capriccio, piano & orchestra* (perf.)
    C13 *Le chant du rossignol* (perf.)
    H1 *L'histoire du soldat* (perf.)
    H4 *L'histoire du soldat* (Suite) (perf.)
    M1 *Mass* (perf.)
    N1 *Les noces* (perf.)
    P35 *Pièces, string quartet* (ded.)
    P58 *Pulcinella* (perf.)

S35 *Symphonie de psaumes* (perf.)
S45 *Symphony, E-flat major, op. 1 (1914)* (perf.)

Auden, Wystan Hugh
   E5 *Elegy for J. F. K.* (text)
   R3 *The rake's progress* (text)

Babin, Victor
   C26 *Circus polka* (arr.)
   P28 *Petroushka: Fête populaire* (arr.)
   P32 *Petroushka: Selections* (arr.)
   T4 *Tango* (arr.)

Babitz, Sol
   C27 *Circus polka* (arr.)

Bach, Johann Sebastian
   Z1 *Von Himmel hoch* (comp.)

Badet, André de
   R3 *The rake's progress* (trans.)

Balanchine, George
   A3 *Agon* (ded.)
   F1 *Fanfare for a new theatre* (ded.)

Ballet Ida Rubenstein
   B3 *Le baiser de la fée* (perf.)
   P9 *Perséphone* (perf.)

Ballet Russe
   M3 *Mavra* (perf.)
   N1 *Les noces* (perf.)
   O5 *Oedipus rex* (perf.)
   O8 *L'oiseau de feu* (perf.)
   P15 *Petroushka* (perf.)
   P58 *Pulcinella* (perf.)
   R7 *Renard* (perf.)
   R13 *Le rossignol* (perf.)
   S1 *Le sacre du printemps* (perf.)

Ballet Society
   O40 *Orpheus* (perf.)

Balmont, Konstantine
   P48 *Poems of Balmont* (text)
   R11 *Le roi des étoiles* (text)

Bartók, Béla
  B1 *Babel* (co-comp.)

Basler Kammerorchester
  C39 *Concerto, string orchestra, D* (perf. & ded.)
  S20 *A sermon, a narrative and a prayer* (perf.)

Beethoven, Ludwig van
  Z2 *Faust: Flohlied* (comp.)

Beliankin, Ludmilla
  P48 *Poems of Balmont* (ded.)

Benois, Alexandre
  P15 *Petroushka* (ded.)
  P17 *Petroushka (1947); piano, 4 hands* (arr.)

Besly, Maurice
  O27 *L'oiseau de feu: La ronde* (arr.)
  O36 *L'oiseau de feu: Selections* (arr.)

Bible
  A1 *Abraham and Isaac* (text)
  B1 *Babel* (text)
  S35 *Symphonie de psaumes* (text)

Biran, Ephraim
  A1 *Abraham and Isaac* (perf.)

Black, Kitty
  H1 *L'histoire du soldat* (trans.)

Bliss, Arthur
  R1 *Ragtime* (perf.)

Bliss, Mr. & Mrs. Robert Woods
  C32 *Concerto, chamber orchestra, E flat* (comm.)

Block, Frederick
  C15 *Le chant du rossignol: Marche chinoise* (arr.)
  O23 *L'oiseau de feu: Danse infernale* (arr.)
  O37 *L'oiseau de feu: Selections* (arr.)
  O38 *L'oiseau de feu: Supplications* (arr.)
  P6 *Pastorale* (arr.)
  P20 *Petroushka: Chez Petrouchka* (arr.)
  P28 *Petroushka: Fête populaire* (arr.)
  R16 *Le rossignol: Chant du rossignol* (arr.)
  S4 *Le sacre du printemps: Les augures printaniers* (arr.)

S5 *Le sacre du printemps: Danse des adolescents* (arr.)
S7 *Le sacre du printemps: Jeux des cités rivales* (arr.)
S8 *Le sacre du printemps: Ronde printanière* (arr.)

Blumenfeld, Felix
C17 *Chant funèbre sur la morte de Rimsky-Korsakov* (perf.)
F2 *Le faune et la bergère* (perf.)
S44 *Symphony, E-flat major, op. 1* (perf.)

Bogomolov, I.
P27 *Petroushka: Danse russe* (arr.)

Boston Symphony Orchestra
C24 *Circus polka* (perf.)
G1 *Greeting prelude* (perf.)
N3 *Norwegian moods* (perf.)
O4 *Ode* (perf.)
P61 *Pulcinella (Suite)* (perf.)
S35 *Symphonie de psaumes* (ded.)

Boulanger, Nadia
C32 *Concerto, chamber orchestra, E-flat* (perf.)
S24 *Sonata, 2 pianos* (perf.)

Brandta, A.
P51 *Poésie de la lyrique japonaise* (text)

Branscomb, Gena
O22 *L'oiseau de feu: Berceuse* (text)

Brown, Maurice
O35 *L'oiseau de feu: Selections* (arr.)

Burness, Robert
M3 *Mavra* (trans.)
M7 *Mavra: Drug moĭ milyĭ* (trans.)
P13 *Petites chansons* (trans.)
P51 *Poésie de la lyrique japonaise* (trans.)

Burt, Julia A.
C28 *Concertino, string quartet* (ed.)
C29 *Concertino, string quartet; piano, 4 hands* (ed.)

CBC Symphony Orchestra
C1 *Canon on a Russian popular theme* (perf.)
I3 *Instrumental miniatures* (perf.)

CBS Television
  F7 *The flood* (perf.)

Calvocoressi, Michel D.
  M11 *Mélodies, op. 6* (trans.)
  P45 *Poèmes de Verlaine, op. 9* (trans.)
  P48 *Poems of Balmont* (trans.)
  R11 *Le roi des étoiles* (trans.)
  R14 *Le rossignol (1962)* (trans.)

Casella, Alfredo
  P36 *Pièces faciles, piano, 4 hands (1915)* (ded.)

Castelnuovo-Tedesco, Mario
  B1 *Babel* (co-comp.)

Chaĭkovskiĭ, Petr
  B3 *Le baiser de la fée* (co-comp. & ded.)
  M3 *Mavra* (ded.)
  Z3 *The sleeping beauty* (co-comp.)
  Z4 *The sleeping beauty* (co-comp.)

Chicago Symphony Orchestra
  S43 *Symphony, C* (ded., perf.)

Chopin, Fryderyk Franciszek
  Z6 *Nocturne* (co-comp.)
  Z7 *Valse brillante* (co-comp.)

Cocteau, Jean
  O5 *Oedipus rex* (text)

Congria, Charles-Albert
  P12 *Petit ramusianum harmonique* (text)

Copeland, George
  O18 *L'oiseau de feu: Berceuse* (arr.)

Craft, Robert
  A1 *Abraham and Isaac* (perf.)
  A3 *Agon* (perf.)
  C1 *Canon on a Russian popular theme* (perf.)
  C22 *Les cinq doigts: Pesante* (perf.)
  D5 *The dove descending breaks the air* (perf.)
  E5 *Elegy for J. F. K.* (perf.)
  I1 *In memoriam Dylan Thomas* (perf.)
  M3 *Mavra* (trans.)

P48 *Poems of Balmont* (trans.)
P54 *Praeludium, jazz ensemble* (perf.)
R13 *Le rossignol* (trans.)
R14 *Le rossignol (1962)* (trans.)
R20 *Russian peasant songs* (perf.)
S1 *Le sacre du printemps* (ed.)
S25 *Songs (1954)* (perf. & trans.)
S26 *Songs from William Shakespeare* (perf.)
T2 *Tango* (perf.)
V3 *Variations, orchestra* (perf.)

Craig, D. Millar
  N1 *Les noces* (trans.)

Cummings, Edward Estlin
  O6 *Oedipus rex (1948)* (trans.)

Cushing, Charles
  Z17 *Smith: The star-spangled banner* (arr.)

Dahl, Ingolf
  D2 *Danses concertantes* (arr.)
  S10 *Scènes de ballet* (arr.)

Daniélou, J.
  O5 *Oedipus rex* (trans.)

Debussy, Claude
  R11 *Le roi des étoiles* (ded.)
  S39 *Symphonies d'instruments à vent* (ded.)

Delage, Maurice
  P51 *Poésie de la lyrique japonaise* (trans. & ded.)

Dickinson, Clarence
  O27 *L'oiseau de feu: La ronde* (arr.)

Diaghilev, Serge
  N1 *Les noces* (ded.)
  O8 *L'oiseau de feu* (comm.)
  P36 *Pièces faciles, piano, 4 hands (1915)* (ded.)

Dufy, Raoul
  D4 *Double canon, string quartet* (ded.)

Dumbarton Oaks Research Library and Collection
  S17 *Septet, piano, winds & strings* (ded.)

Dushkin, Samuel
  B8 *Le baiser de la fée (Suite)* (arr.)
  B10 *Le baiser de la fée: Deuxième tabeau: Selection* (arr.)
  C16 *Le chant du rossignol: Selections* (arr.)
  C41 *Concerto, violin, D major* (ed. & perf.)
  C42 *Concerto, violin, D major; violin & piano* (arr.)
  D7 *Duo concertante* (perf.)
  M5 *Mavra: Drug moĭ milyĭ* (arr.)
  O15 *L'oiseau de feu: Berceuse* (arr.)
  O33 *L'oiseau de feu: Scherzo* (arr.)
  P2 *Pastorale* (arr.)
  P4 *Pastorale* (arr.)
  P23 *Petroushka: Danse russe* (arr.)
  S33 *Suite italienne, violin & piano* (arr.)
  T5 *Tango* (arr.)

Eliot, Thomas Stearns
  D5 *The dove descending breaks the air* (text)
  I4 *Introitus* (ded.)

Elukhen, A.
  M3 *Mavra* (trans.)
  R13 *Le rossignol* (trans.)
  R14 *Le rossignol (1962)* (trans.)

Erickson, Frank
  W4 *Works, piano, 4 hands: Selections* (arr.)

Errazuriz, Eugenia
  E7 *Etude, piano* (ded.)
  P41 *Pièces faciles, piano, 4 hands (1917)* (ded.)
  R1 *Ragtime* (ded.)

Evans, Merle
  C25 *Circus polka* (perf.)

Fairchild, Blair
  C41 *Concerto, violin, D major* (comm.)

Feiwel, Berthold
  P48 *Poems of Balmont* (trans.)
  R13 *Le rossignol* (trans.)
  R14 *Le rossignol (1962)* (trans.)

Fitelberg, Gregor
  M3 *Mavra* (perf.)

Flanders, Michael
    H1 *L'histoire du soldat* (trans.)

Flonzaley Quartet
    C28 *Concertino, string quartet*

Forst, Rudolf
    O20 *L'oiseau de feu: Berceuse* (arr.)
    O29 *L'oiseau de feu: La ronde* (arr.)

Funkorchester, Berlin
    C41 *Concerto, violin, D major* (perf.)

Gardner, Maurice
    O16 *L'oiseau de feu: Berceuse* (arr.)
    P30 *Petroushka: Selections* (arr.)

Gautier, Jeanne
    B11 *Le baiser de la fée: Deuxième tableau: Selection* (arr.)

Gesualdo, Carlo
    M12 *Monumentum pro Gesualdo de Venosa ad CD annum* (co-comp.)
    Z8 *Gesualdo: Sacrae cantiones* (co-comp.)

Gide, André
    P9 *Perséphone* (text)

Gilajew, A.
    S46 *Symphony, E-flat major, op. 1* (arr.)

Glinka, Mikhail Ivanovich
    M3 *Mavra* (ded.)

Gontcharova, Natalie
    B13 *Berceuses du chat* (ded.)

Goodman, Benny
    T3 *Tango* (perf.)

Gorodetzky, S.
    M11 *Mélodies, op. 6* (text)

Greissle, Felix
    R19 *Russian peasant songs* (arr.)

Grieg, Edvard Hagerup
    Z9 *Grieg: Kobald* (co-comp.)

Grovlez, Gabriel
  S16 *Scherzo fantastique* (arr.)

Guenther, Felix
  P25 *Petroushka: Danse russe* (arr.)
  P26 *Petroushka: Danse russe* (arr.)
  T3 *Tango* (arr.)

Hamm, Charles E.
  P15 *Petroushka* (ed.)

Hayne, Charles C.
  R13 *Le rossignol* (trans.)

Hendl, Walter
  E1 *Ebony concerto* (perf.)

Herman, Woody
  E1 *Ebony concerto* (perf.)

Hindemith, Paul
  B1 *Babel* (co-comp.)

Hirschfeld, Max
  E13 *Etudes, piano, op. 7: no. 4* (ed.)

Hoffmann, R. St.
  B13 *Berceuses du chat* (trans.)
  P56 *Pribaoutki* (trans.)

Huxley, Aldous
  V3 *Variations, orchestra* (ded.)

Hylton, Jack
  M10 *Mavra: Selections* (arr. & perf.)

Israel, The people of
  A1 *Abraham and Isaac* (ded.)

Isaac, Merle J.
  O35 *L'oiseau de feu: Selections* (arr.)

Iturbi, José
  P33 *Piano-rag music* (perf.)
  P36 *Pièces faciles, piano, 4 hands (1915)* (perf.)
  P41 *Pièces faciles, piano, 4 hands (1917)* (perf.)

Janssen, Werner
    B1 *Babel* (perf.)
    D1 *Danses concertantes* (perf.)

Johnson, Richard
    S24 *Sonata, 2 pianos* (perf.)

Kallman, Chester
    R3 *The rake's progress* (text)

Kennedy, John Fitzgerald
    E5 *Elegy for J. F. K.* (ded.)

Kibalchich, Vassily
    R19 *Russian peasant songs* (perf.)

Kireivsky,
    N1 *Les noces* (text)

Kirstein, Lincoln
    A3 *Agon* (ded.)
    F1 *Fanfare for a new theatre* (ded.)

Klenner, John
    O31 *L'oiseau de feu: La ronde* (text)

Kochanski, Paul
    O14 *L'oiseau de feu: Berceuse* (ded.)
    O33 *L'oiseau de feu: Scherzo* (ded.)
    O34 *L'oiseau de feu: Selections* (ded.)
    S32 *Suite, violin & piano* (ded.)

Kochno, Boris
    M3 *Mavra* (text)

Koller, Rupert
    R7 *Renard* (trans.)

Komaroff, A.
    F2 *Le faune et la bergère* (trans.)

Koussevitsky, Natalie
    C34 *Concerto, piano & band* (ded.)
    O4 *Ode, orchestra* (ded.)

Koussevitsky, Serge
    C34 *Concerto, piano & band* (perf.)
    O4 *Ode, orchestra* (comm. & perf.)

     S35 *Symphonie de psaumes* (comm.)
     S39 *Symphonies d'instruments à vent* (perf.)

Küfferle, Rinaldo
     R3 *The rake's progress* (trans.)

Larionov, Michel
     B13 *Berceuses du chat* (ded.)

Larmanjat, Jacques
     M3 *Mavra* (trans.)

Lear, Edward
     O42 *The owl and the pussy cat* (text)

Lester, William
     O32 *L'oiseau de feu: La ronde* (arr.)
     P21 *Petroushka: Danse de la ballerine* (arr.)
     P22 *Petroushka: Danse des cochers* (arr.)

Lisle, Claude Joseph Rouget de
     Z10 *Lisle: La marseillaise* (co-comp.)

Los Angeles Chamber Symphony Orchestra and Society
     C3 *Cantata* (perf. & ded.)
     C30 *Concertino, string quartet; winds & strings* (perf.)

Lourié, Arthur
     C31 *Concertino, string quartet* (arr.)
     O3 *Octet, winds* (arr.)
     S41 *Symphonies d'instruments à vent* (arr.)

Maganini, Quinto
     O17 *L'oiseau de feu: Berceuse* (arr.)
     O19 *L'oiseau de feu: Berceuse* (arr.)
     O20 *L'oiseau de feu: Berceuse* (arr.)
     O21 *L'oiseau de feu: Berceuse* (arr.)
     O29 *L'oiseau de feu: La ronde* (arr.)
     P5 *Pastorale* (arr.)
     P18 *Petroushka* (arr.)

Markevitch, Dmitri
     M6 *Mavra: Drug moĭ milyĭ* (arr.)

Max Egon, Prince of Fürstenberg
     E6 *Epitaphium* (ded.)

Meung, Jean de
  L1 *Little canon* (text)

Meyers, Rollo M.
  R7 *Renard* (trans.)

Milhaud, Darius
  B1 *Babel* (co-comp.)

Mirkina, M.
  P19 *Petroushka* (arr.)

Mitusov, E.
  E12 *Etudes, piano, op. 7* (ded.)

Mitusov, S.
  P45 *Poèmes de Verlaine, op. 9* (trans.)
  R13 *Le rossignol* (text & ded.)

Möller, Heinrich
  F2 *Le faune et la bergère* (trans.)

Monteux, Pierre
  G1 *Greeting prelude* (ded.)
  P15 *Petroushka* (perf.)
  P61 *Pulcinella (Suite)* (perf.)
  R13 *Le rossignol* (perf.)
  S1 *Le sacre du printemps* (perf.)

Morton, Laurence
  I3 *Instrumental miniatures* (ded.)

Munch, Charles
  G1 *Greeting prelude* (perf.)

Musorgskiĭ, Modest Petrovich
  Z11 *Musorgskiĭ: Boris Godunov: Prologue* (co-comp.)
  Z12 *Musorgskiĭ: Khovanshchina: Selections* (co-comp.)
  Z13 *Musorgskiĭ: Pesnia o blokhe* (co-comp.)

Nelson, Robert E.
  E2 *Ebony concerto* (arr.)

Newmarch, Rosa
  H1 *L'histoire du soldat* (trans.)
  S25 *Songs (1954)* (trans.)

New York Philarmonic-Symphony Society
S47 *Symphony (1945)* (perf. & ded.)

Norddeutscher Rundfunk
T6 *Threni* (ded.)

Norman, Theodore
C21 *Les cinq doigts* (arr.)
C21.5 *Les cinq doigts: Allegro* (arr.)

Orchestre de la Suisse Romande
C13 *Le chant du rossignol* (perf.)

Oistrakh, David
C42 *Concerto, violin, D major* (ed.)

Onnou, Alphonse
E3 *Elegy, viola* (ded.)

Paris Symphony Orchestra
C7 *Capriccio, piano & orchestra* (perf.)

Pavchinskogo, S.
P19 *Petroushka* (arr.)

Pergolesi, Giovanni Battista
P58 *Pulcinella* (co-comp.)
S32 *Suite, violin & piano* (co-comp.)

Petrenko, Elizabeth
M11 *Mélodies, op. 6* (perf.)

Philharmonic Quartet, London
R1 *Ragtime* (perf.)

Piatigorsky, Gregor
S34 *Suite italienne, violoncello & piano* (arr.)

Pierné, Gabriel
O8 *L'oiseau de feu* (cond.)

Piper, Brook P.
O27 *L'oiseau de feu: La ronde* (arr.)

Polignac, Princess Edmond de
R7 *Renard* (ded.)
S23 *Sonata, piano* (ded.)

Popular Russian texts
- B13 *Berceuses du chat*
- C18 *Chants russes*
- H8 *Histoires pour enfants*
- P13 *Petites chansons*
- P56 *Pribaoutki*
- N1 *Les noces*
- R7 *Renard*
- R19 *Russian peasant songs*

Prévost, Germain
- E3 *Elegie, viola* (comm.)

Prokof'ev, Sergeĭ
- B1 *Babel* (co-comp.)
- P27 *Petroushka: Danse russe*

Pushkin, Alexander
- F2 *Le faune et la bergère* (text)
- M3 *Mavra*

Raiz, Aladar
- P39 *Pièces faciles, piano, 4 hands (1915): Polka* (ded.)

Ramuz, C. F.
- B12 *Berceuse* (text)
- B13 *Berceuses du chat* (trans.)
- C18 *Chants russes* (trans.)
- H1 *L'histoire du soldat* (text)
- H8 *Histoires pour enfants* (trans.)
- N1 *Les noces* (trans.)
- P12 *Petit ramusianum harmonique* (ded.)
- P13 *Petites chansons* (trans.)
- P56 *Pribaoutki* (trans.)
- R7 *Renard* (trans.)

Ravel, Maurice
- P51 *Poèsie de la lyrique japonaise* (ded.)

Reinhart, Hans
- H1 *L'histoire du soldat* (trans.)

Reinhart, Werner
- H1 *L'histoire du soldat* (ded.)
- P34 *Pièces, clarinet* (ded.)

Reskin, David
   C25 *Circus polka* (arr.)

Richter, Nicolas
   E12 *Etudes, piano, op. 7* (ded.)
   S22 *Sonata, piano (1904)* (ded. & perf.)

Ringling Brothers, Barnum and Bailey Circus
   C24 *Circus polka* (comm.)
   C25 *Circus polka* (perf.)

Rimskiĭ-Korsakov, Andrei
   E12 *Etudes, piano, op. 7* (ded.)
   O8 *L'oiseau de feu* (ded.)

Rimskiĭ-Korsakov, Nadezhda
   P1 *Pastorale* (ded.)

Rimskiĭ-Korsakov, Nikolai
   C17 *Chant funèbre sur la morte de Rimsky-Korsakov, op. 5* (ded.)
   S44 *Symphony, E-flat major, op. 1* (ded.)

Rimskiĭ-Korsakov, Vladimir
   E12 *Etudes, piano, op. 7* (ded.)

Roepper, Charles
   O18 *L'oiseau de feu: Berceuse* (arr.)

Roerich, Nicolas
   S1 *Le sacre du printemps* (ded.)

Rose, Billy
   S9 *Scènes de ballet* (comm.)

Roth, Ernst
   P51 *Poésie de la lyrique japonaise* (trans.)

Roth, Hermann
   R19 *Russian peasant songs* (trans.)

Roux, Dr.
   C2 *Canons, 2 horns* (ded.)

Russian Symphony Orchestra
   F2 *Le faune et la bergère* (perf.)
   S44 *Symphony, E-flat major, op. 1* (perf.)

Rubinstein, Artur
    P29 *Petroushka: Selections* (ded.)
    P33 *Piano-rag music* (ded.)

Rubinstein, Ida
    B3 *Le baiser de la fée* (perf.)
    P9 *Perséphone* (perf.)

Sacher, Paul
    C39 *Concerto, string orchestra, D* (ded. & perf.)
    S20 *A sermon, a narrative and a prayer* (ded. & perf.)

San Francisco Symphony Orchestra
    S12 *Scherzo à la russe* (perf.)

Satie, Erik
    P36 *Pièces faciles, piano, 4 hands (1915)* (ded.)

Schilkret, Nathaniel
    B1 *Babel* (co-comp. & comm.)

Schmitt, Florent
    P51 *Poésie de la lyrique japonaise* (ded.)

Schneider, F. H.
    P35 *Pièces, string quartet* (ed.)

Schönberg, Arnold
    B1 *Babel* (co-comp.)

Schroeder, Fritz
    R3 *The rake's progress* (trans.)

Shakespeare, William
    S26 *Songs from William Shakespeare* (text)
    S27 *Songs from William Shakespeare; voice & piano* (text)

Sibelius, Jean
    Z14 *Sibelius: Canzonetta* (co-comp.)

Siloti, Alexandre
    F4 *Feu d'artifice, op. 4* (perf.)
    S15 *Scherzo fantastique* (ded. & perf.)

Singer, Lou
    O31 *L'oiseau de feu: La ronde* (arr.)

Singer, Otto
    F6 *Feu d'artifice* (arr.)

Smith, John Stafford
 Z15 *Smith: The star-spangled banner; arr., orchestra* (co-comp.)
 Z16 *Smith: The star-spangled banner; piano-vocal score* (co-comp.)
 Z17 *Smith: The star-spangled banner; arr., band* (co-comp.)

Société Musicale Indépendante
 P51 *Poésie de la lyrique japonaise* (perf.)

Société Philharmonique de Bruxelles
 S35 *Symphonie de psaumes* (perf.)

Spaulding, Albert
 C34 *Concerto, piano & band* (ed.)
 C36 *Concerto, piano & band; 2 pianos* (ed.)
 M4 *Mavra; piano-vocal score* (arr.)
 O1 *Octet, winds* (ed.)
 P61 *Pulcinella (Suite)* (ed.)
 S19 *Serenade, piano, A* (ed.)
 S23 *Sonata, piano (1924)* (ed.)

Spinner, Leopold
 M2 *Mass* (arr.)
 O41 *Orpheus* (arr.)

Steinberg, Nadia & Maximilian
 F4 *Feu d'artifice, op. 4* (ded.)

Stone, Gregory
 H6 *L'histoire du soldat: Devil's dance* (arr.)
 P42 *Pièces faciles, piano, 4 hands (1915): Napolitana* (arr.)

Stott, John
 E10 *Etudes, orchestra: Cantique* (arr.)

Stravinsky, Anna Kholodvsky
 P48 *Poems of Balmont* (ded.)

Stravinsky, Ekaterina Gabrielovna
 F2 *Le faune et la bergère* (ded.)
 P56 *Pribaoutki* (ded.)
 S19 *Serenade, piano, A* (ded.)

Stravinsky, Gury
 P45 *Poèmes de Verlaine, op. 9* (ded.)

Stravinsky, Igor
 B3 *Le basier de la fée* (perf.)

Stravinsky, Vera (de Bosset)
    O1 *Octet, winds* (ded.)

Strozzi-Pečić, Béla & Maja de
    C18 *Chants russes* (ded.)

Sucra, Luis
    P24 *Petroushka: Danse russe* (arr.)

Szántó, Théodore
    P31 *Petroushka: Selections* (arr.)
    R17 *Le rossignol: Marche chinoise* (arr.)

Tansman, Alexandre
    B1 *Babel* (co-comp.)

Teatro alla Scala, Orchestra & Chorus
    R3 *The rake's progress* (perf.)

Teatro La Fenice, Orchestra
    M12 *Monumentum pro Gesualdo de Venosa ad CD annum* (perf.)

Thomas, Dylan
    I1 *In memoriam Dylan Thomas* (ded.)
    I2 *In memoriam Dylan Thomas; voice & piano* (ded.)

Thurneiser, L.
    O5 *Oedipus rex* (trans.)

Timothieff, Basil T.
    R13 *Le rossignol* (trans.)

Toch, Ernst
    B1 *Babel* (co-comp.)

Tschaikowsky, Peter
    see Chaĭkovskiĭ, Petr

Verlaine, Paul
    P45 *Poèmes de Verlaine, op. 9* (text)

Weber, Margrit
    M13 *Movements, piano & orchestra* (perf. & ded.)

Weinhold, Liesbeth
    R13 *Le rossignol* (trans.)

Werner Janssen Orchestra of Los Angeles
    B1 *Babel* (perf.)
    D1 *Danses concertantes* (perf. & comm.)

Wharton, Edith
  S28 *Souvenir d'une marche boche*

White, Eric Walter
  V2 *Valse pour les enfants*

Whiteman, Paul
  S11 *Scherzo à la russe* (ded. & perf.)

Willms, Franz
  O18 *L'oiseau de feu: Berceuse* (arr.)
  O28 *L'oiseau de feu: La ronde* (arr.)

Wolf, Hugo
  Z18 *Spanisches Liederbuch: Selections* (co-comp.)

4. *Chronological index*

Reference is made to the index number of the main entries by the year in which the work indicated was completed. Arrangements by other figures are not included.

1904:
  M15 *The mushrooms going to war*
  S22 *Sonata, piano (1904)*

1906:
  F2 *Le faune et la bergère, op. 2*

1907:
  P1 *Pastorale*
  S44 *Symphony, E-flat major, op. 1*

1908:
  C17 *Chant funèbre sur la morte de Rimsky-Korsakov, op. 5*
  E12 *Etudes, piano, op. 7*
  F4 *Feu d'artifice, op. 4*
  M11 *Mélodies, op. 6*
  S15 *Scherzo fantastique, op. 3*

1909:

    Z6 *Chopin: Nocturne; arr.*
    Z7 *Chopin: Valse brillante; arr.*
    Z9 *Grieg: Kobald; arr.*

1910:

    O8 *L'oiseau de feu*
    O9 *L'oiseau de feu; piano*
    P45 *Poèmes de Verlaine, op. 9*
    Z2 *Beethoven: Faust: Flohlied; arr.*
    Z13 *Musorgskiĭ: Pesnia o blokhe; arr.*

1911:

    O10 *L'oiseau de feu (Suite)*
    P15 *Petroushka*
    P48 *Poems of Balmont*

1912:

    R11 *Le roi des étoiles*

1913:

    P13 *Petites chansons*
    P51 *Poésie de la lyrique japonaise*
    S1 *Le sacre du printemps*
    Z12 *Musorgskiĭ: Khovanshchina: Selections; arr.*

1914:

    P35 *Pièces, string quartet*
    P56 *Pribaoutki*
    R13 *Le rossignol*
    S45 *Symphony, E-flat major, op. 1 (1914)*
    V1 *Valse des fleurs*

1915:

    P36 *Pièces faciles, piano, 4 hands (1915)*
    P37 *Pièces faciles, piano, 4 hands (1915): March*
    P39 *Pièces faciles, piano, 4 hands (1915): Polka*
    S28 *Souvenir d'une marche boche*

1916:

    B13 *Berceuses du chat*
    R7 *Renard*

1917:

    B12 *Berceuse*
    C2 *Canons, 2 horns*

C13 *Le chant du rossignol*
D3 *Dialogue between reason and joy*
E7 *Etude, piano*
H8 *Histoires pour enfants*
P41 *Pièces faciles, piano, 4 hands (1917)*
R19 *Russian peasant songs*
V2 *Valse pour les enfants*
Z5 *Chant des bateliers du Volga; arr.*

1918:

D6 *Duet, bassoons*
H1 *L'histoire du soldat*
R1 *Ragtime*
Z11 *Musorgskiĭ: Boris Godunov: Prologue; arr.*

1919:

C18 *Chants russes*
H5 *L'histoire du soldat (Suite)*
O11 *L'oiseau de feu (Suite, 1919)*
P33 *Piano-rag music*
P34 *Pieces, clarinet*
R2 *Ragtime; piano*
Z10 *Lisle: La marseillaise*

1920:

C28 *Concertino, string quartet*
C29 *Concertino, string quartet; piano, 4 hands*
P58 *Pulcinella*
P61 *Pulcinella (Suite)*
S39 *Symphonies d'instruments à vent*

1921:

C20 *Les cinq doigts*
P29 *Petroushka: Selections; piano*
S31 *Suite, orchestra, no. 2*
Z3 *Chaĭkovskiĭ: The sleeping beauty: Selections; arr.*

1922:

M3 *Mavra*

1923:

H10 *Histoires pour enfants: Tilimbom; voice & orchestra*
N1 *Les noces*
O1 *Octet, winds*
P3 *Pastorale; soprano, oboe, English horn, clarinet, bassoon*

1924:

    C34 *Concerto, piano & band*
    C36 *Concerto, piano & band; 2 pianos*
    S23 *Sonata, piano (1924)*

1925.

    S19 *Serenade, piano, A*
    S30 *Suite, orchestra, no. 1*
    S32 *Suite, violin & piano*

1926:

    P7 *Pater noster*

1927:

    O5 *Oedipus rex*

1928:

    A5 *Apollon musagète*
    B3 *Le baiser de la fée*
    E8 *Etudes, orchestra*

1929:

    C7 *Capriccio, piano & orchestra*
    O14 *L'oiseau de feu: Berceuse; violin & piano*
    O34 *L'oiseau de feu: Selections; violin & piano*

1930:

    P14 *Petites chansons; voice & orchestra*
    S35 *Symphonie de psaumes*

1930 ca.:

    C19 *Church prayer*
    S36 *Symphonie de psaumes; piano-vocal score*

1931:

    C41 *Concerto, violin, D major*

1932:

    B8 *Le baiser de la fée (Suite); violin & piano*
    C16 *Le chant du rossignol: Selections; violin & piano*
    C43 *Credo*
    D7 *Duo concertante, violin & piano*
    P23 *Petroushka: Danse russe; violin & piano*
    O15 *L'oiseau de feu: Berceuse; violin & piano (1932)*
    S34 *Suite italienne, violoncello & piano*

1933:

    O33 *L'oiseau de feu: Scherzo; violin & piano*
    P2 *Pastorale; oboe, English horn, Clarinet, bassoon & violin*
    P4 *Pastorale; violin & piano*

1933 ca.:

    S33 *Suite italienne, violin & piano*

1934:

    A8 *Ave Marie*
    B10 *Le baiser de la fée: Deuxième tableau: Selection (1934)*
    P9 *Perséphone*

1935:

    C38 *Concerto, 2 pianos*

1936:

    C11 *The card party*

1937:

    B7 *Le baiser de la fée (Suite)*
    M5 *Mavra: Drug moĭ milyĭ; violin & piano*
    P12 *Petit ramusianum harmonique*
    P53 *Praeludium, jazz ensemble*

1938:

    C32 *Concerto, chamber orchestra, E flat*

1940:

    S43 *Symphony, C*
    T1 *Tango, piano*

1941:

    Z4 *Chaĭkovskiĭ: The sleeping beauty: Selections; arr.*
    Z15 *Smith: The star-spangled banner; arr.*

1942:

    C23 *Circus polka; piano*
    C24 *Circus polka; orchestra*
    D1 *Danses concertantes*
    N3 *Norwegian moods*

1943:

    O4 *Ode, orchestra*
    S6 *Le sacre du printemps: Danse sacrale (1943)*

1944:

    B1 *Babel*

    E3 *Elegie, viola*

    S9 *Scènes de ballet*

    S11 *Scherzo à la russe*

    S12 *Scherzo à la russe; orchestra*

    S24 *Sonata, 2 pianos*

1945:

    E1 *Ebony concerto*

    O12 *L'oiseau de feu (Suite, 1945)*

    S47 *Symphony (1945)*

1946:

    C39 *Concerto, string orchestra, D*

    P16 *Petroushka (1947)*

1946 ca.:

    C40 *Concerto, string orchestra, D (revised)*

1947:

    A7 *Apollon musagète (1947)*

    L1 *Little canon*

    M7 *Mavra: Drug moĭ milyĭ; voice & piano*

    O40 *Orpheus*

    P49 *Poems of Balmont (revised)*

    P62 *Pulcinella (Suite, 1947)*

    S40 *Symphonies d'instruments à vent (1947)*

1948:

    M1 *Mass*

    O6 *Oedipus rex (1948)*

    S37 *Symphonie de psaumes (1948)*

1949:

    A9 *Ave Marie (1949)*

    B9 *Le baiser de la fée (Suite, 1949)*

    C9 *Capriccio, piano & orchestra (1949)*

    C10 *Capriccio, piano & orchestra (1949); 2 pianos*

    C44 *Credo (1949)*

    P8 *Pater noster (1949)*

    P10 *Perséphone (1949)*

    P63 *Pulcinella (Suite, 1949)*

1950:
- B5 *Le baiser de la fée (1950)*
- C35 *Concerto, piano & band (1950)*

1951:
- B11 *Le baiser de la fée: Deuxième tableau: Selection (1951)*
- P47 *Poèmes de Verlaine, op. 9; voice & orchestra*
- R3 *The rake's progress*

1952:
- C3 *Cantata*
- C30 *Concertino, string quartet; winds & strings*
- E9 *Etudes, orchestra (1952)*
- O2 *Octet, winds (1952)*

1953:
- P46 *Poèmes de Verlaine, op. 9 (1953)*
- P54 *Praeludium, jazz ensemble (1953)*
- S17 *Septet, piano, winds & strings*
- S26 *Songs from William Shakespeare*
- T2 *Tango; piano; orchestra*

1954:
- I1 *In memoriam Dylan Thomas*
- I2 *In memorian Dylan Thomas; voice & piano*
- P50 *Poems of Balmont; voice & chamber orchestra*
- R20 *Russian peasant songs; women's voices & 4 horns*
- S25 *Songs (1954)*

1955:
- C5 *Canticum sacrum*
- G1 *Greeting prelude*

1956:
- Z1 *Bach: Von Himmel hoch; arr.*

1957:
- A3 *Agon*
- Z8 *Gesualdo: Sacrae cantiones; arr.*

1958:
- T6 *Threni*

1959:
- D4 *Double canon, string quartet*
- E6 *Epitaphium*

ST. PETER'S COLLEGE LIBRARY

3 6980 00202 0726

016.780424
ST8

M13 *Movements, piano & orchestra*
M14 *Movements, piano & orchestra; 2 pianos*

1960:

M12 *Monumentum pro Gesualdo de Venosa ad CD annum*

1961:

C22 *Les cinq doigts: Pesante, instrumental ensemble*
S20 *A sermon, a narrative and a prayer*

1962:

D5 *The dove descending breaks the air*
F7 *The flood*
I3 *Instrumental miniatures, winds & strings*
R14 *Le rossignol (1962)*

1963:

A1 *Abraham and Isaac*
Z14 *Sibelius: Canzonetta; arr.*

1964:

C45 *Credo (1964)*
E5 *Elegy for J. F. K.*
F1 *Fanfare for a new theatre*
V3 *Variations, orchestra*

1965:

C1 *Canon on a Russian popular theme*
I4 *Introitus*
P59 *Pulcinella (1965)*

1966:

O42 *The owl and the pussy cat*
R9 *Requiem canticles*

1968:

Z18 *Wolf: Spanisches Liederbuch: Selections; arr.*